Dear student,

Now you're in 'Klasse 10', it's time to start looking more closely at the skills you'll need to be successful in your final exam – even though that might feel like a long way away. The idea of this *Language and Skills Trainer* is to help you develop and practise every skill you need and also to introduce you to exam-like assignments.

In Part A, *First check*, the tasks are very close to the ones you will have to deal with in class tests this year. Exercises guide you step-by-step through each task. What can you do if you find you need more practice with some of the skills required in the tasks? References in the margin lead you to relevant pages of exercises in Part B, *Language and skills*, where you will find additional help and tips for each task. Of course, you can also work on the exercises in Part B independently of Part A.

When you're confident that you have mastered Parts A and B, you can move on to Part C, *Test yourself*, which contains two revision sections and two mock exams to be done during the school year and a set of activities for developing your speaking skills for test purposes. In the mock exams, which are based on common class test formats for 'Klasse 10', different skills come together.

You will have noticed that the *Language and Skills Trainer* does not follow the structure of your *Green Line 6 Transition* Pupil's Book. Instead, it is organized according to the CORE SKILLS you can find in each Topic. In this way, the *Trainer* is closely connected to the Skills section of the Pupil's Book. At every stage of your work with the *Trainer* there are references to the relevant skills, all of them also being used while you work through *Green Line 6 Transition*. The topics covered in the *Trainer* are all ones you will find in the Pupil's Book.

You can use the *Language and Skills Trainer* both in the classroom and at home. This means you can concentrate on your individual weak spots in private, but also work with others where partner or group work is an advantage. The CDs at the back of the book contain a) all the videos and the listening texts (playable both on your computer and on a CD player) plus transcripts, and the solutions for the exercises in each part of the *Language and Skills Trainer*, and b) all the videos and the listening texts plus transcripts for the exercises in your *Green Line 6 Transition* Pupil's Book, together with the Vocabulary sheets for all the Topics and texts in your Pupil's Book.

All the best for your work in English this year!

Your *Green Line* Team

Symbolerklärung

- Write on a separate sheet of paper.
- Do this task with another person.
- Do this task in a (small) group.
- This listening text is on the CD-ROM in this book.
- This film clip is on the CD-ROM in this book.
- →S3 Look at Skill 3 in your Pupil's Book.
- →p. 65 For further practice, go to this page in your *Language and Skills Trainer*.

Inhalt

A First check

B Language and skills

C Test yourself

Reading skills

→S1, S2

Reading for gist and for detail

When you are confronted with an unfamiliar text, additional information is sometimes given in an illustration or headline. This is not the case with the first text which you are going to read.

1 *Find out about the genre of the text. What types of text can you rule out when you first look at it, even before you read it? Now read it once quickly. What type of text is it? Fiction or non-fiction? A review? A biography? An advertisement? Make notes.*

→p. 20, p. 21

2 *Read the text for gist. (This process is also known as skimming.) Sum up the most important information in the text in one or two sentences.*

In research published today in the journal *Cognitive Development*, children, adolescents and adults aged 9–35 years chose between risky and safe options in a computer gambling game. Scientists found that the teenagers took the most risks compared with the other groups, with the most risky behaviour seen in 14-year-olds.

The results suggest that teenagers are good at weighing up the pros and cons of their decisions (unlike children), but take risks because they enjoy the thrill of a risky situation more than other age groups – especially when they have a 'lucky escape'.

"The reason that teenagers take risks is not a problem with foreseeing the consequences. It was more because they chose to take those risks," said Dr Stephanie Burnett from the UCL Institute of Cognitive Neuroscience, and the lead author.

"This is the first evidence from a lab-based study that adolescents are risk-takers. We are one step forward in determining why teenagers engage in extremely risky behaviours such as drug use and unsafe sex," she added.

The study involved 86 boys and men who were asked to play computer games, during which they made decisions in order to win points. After each game scientists measured the participants' emotional response by recording how satisfied or dissatisfied they were with the outcome.

They found that the onset of the teenage years marked an increase in how much enjoyment resulted from winning in a 'lucky escape' situation. This could help explain why teenagers are more likely to take bigger risks.

"The onset of adolescence marks an explosion in 'risky' activities – from dangerous driving, unsafe sex and experimentation with alcohol, to poor dietary habits and physical inactivity.

"Understanding why adolescents take such risks is important for public health interventions and for families," said Dr Sarah-Jayne Blakemore, also from the UCL Institute for Cognitive Neuroscience, and co-author of the research.

→pp. 22–23

3 [▤] *Now look for more detailed information in the text. (This process is also known as scanning.) Find the answers to these questions.*

> **TIP** Underline the relevant parts of the text before you write your answer.

1. Who took part in the study? What did they do?
2. What did the scientists do?
3. Whose behaviour is most risky?
4. Why do they behave in this way?
5. Who could be interested in the results of the study?

4 [▤] *Explain these phrases from the text in your own words.*

> **TIP** Read the phrases in the context of the text.

1. "a problem with foreseeing the consequences" (ll. 18–19)
2. "a lab-based study" (ll. 24–25)
3. "the onset of the teenage years" (ll. 37–38)
4. "poor dietary habits and physical inactivity" (ll. 46–47)
5. "public health interventions" (ll. 49–50)

Scanning texts for specific information: Biography

→S1
→pp. 22–23

1 [📖] *Read this text about Lady Gaga once and underline all the basic information in it about her family, childhood, education, etc. Make a chronological list, adding the year where possible.*

Lady Gaga is not her real name, of course. – She didn't acquire this stage name until she had started her career as a singer. She was already a successful songwriter at age 20, writing songs for famous acts like the Pussycat Dolls. Soon record producers became impressed by her talent as a vocal performer, and she signed her first contract. That was her chance to create new material for her debut album *The Fame* which was released in 2008. The album included two of her most famous hit singles, *Just Dance* (which was nominated for a Grammy as the Best Dance Recording) and *Poker Face*.

Lady Gaga was born Stefani Joanne Angelina Germanotta in New York in 1986. Both her parents have Italian roots, and maybe they passed on the Italian love of music to their daughter. Little Stefani enjoyed singing and dancing, and she had a talent for performing right from the start. At age four she learned to play the piano and by the time she was 13 she had composed her first piece of music. She went to a Catholic school, the Convent of the Sacred Heart, where she worked hard and enjoyed acting in school plays. School was not the only place she performed. At 14 she started taking part in New York club shows where members of the audience could sing or dance if they wanted to – so-called 'open mic nights'.

At the age of 17, Lady Gaga was admitted to New York University's Tisch School of the Arts to study music, an exceptional honour for someone so young. However, about two years later she dropped out of New York University and left home.

In 2004 she moved to a cheap apartment, determined to get her career as a singer going. She started a band with some friends from New York University and became part of the Lower East Side club scene. She had always been inspired by rock artists like Queen and pop singers such as Madonna and Michael Jackson, and she now wanted to create her own musical style – something different and provocative. She also started to try out drugs and appear in night club shows with transvestites and go-go dancers. Her father was shocked. "He couldn't look at me for a few months," Lady Gaga says, looking back. "He just didn't understand."

2 *Read the text again. Using a different colour underline the phrases about her artistic talents.*

Scanning texts for specific information: A tourist website

→S1
→pp. 22–23

1 *A group of teenagers want to visit Mesa Verde National Park in Colorado, famous for its ancient houses built inside cliffs. They want to know if they can tour the whole site freely and visit all the houses without paying. One of them is also interested in taking photos of the landscape and Native American culture. Scan the text and underline any information which is useful to them.*

In Mesa Verde there are over 4,000 separate historic ruins, many of them large structures built under steep, overhanging cliffs in narrow canyons. This is the most famous and highly visited archaeological site in the US due to the number, the size and the excellent state of preservation of the buildings, together with their scenic location. Today, most of the region is still within Native American reservations.

Approach: Mesa Verde National Park is approached from US 160, which runs along the Montezuma Valley between Cortez and Mancos – there are plenty of interesting Native American souvenir shops in these towns and alongside the road. A turning leads steeply up into the hilly area towards the park. At one point there is a tunnel taking the road between two canyons, and there are several stopping points with great views of the park to the south and north over a huge area of Colorado. On a clear day it is possible to see Shiprock Peak in New Mexico, 50 miles away.

Tours: Some of the most interesting cliff dwellings can only be visited by taking a ranger-guided tour. Tickets must be purchased in advance at the Far View Visitor Center ($3.00 per person). Due to high demand during the summer season, you may be asked to choose only one of the tours per day. One particular favorite is a tour through Balcony House. This one-hour tour involves climbing a 32-ft ladder, crawling through a 12-ft-long tunnel, and climbing up a 60-ft open rock face with two 10-ft ladders to exit the site. The tour begins at the Balcony House parking area, a 25-minute drive from the Visitor Center.

2 [📖] *In your own words summarize the information you have underlined.*

→S1, S6, S7
→pp. 24–25

TIP

In fictional texts the writer does not always want to provide you with information. Feelings and atmosphere are often more important than facts.

Close reading: A fictional text

A close reading of the text is necessary to discover the inner structure, e.g. the development of the narrator's thoughts and feelings.

1 *This text is the beginning of a short story. When you have read it for gist, read it again and underline the relevant information about the narrator.*

When the Wasps Drowned by Clare Wigfall

That was the summer Therese stepped on the wasps' nest, and put an end to our barefoot wanderings; the summer when the sun shone every day and everybody commented upon it, old ladies breathing heavily on park benches, fanning themselves with well-thumbed issues of *Woman's Own*. "Oh, isn't it hot?" they'd sigh, and I, desperate for conversation, would agree and smile and sit high on the wooden seat and imagine myself as old as they were. It was all anyone seemed to speak of that summer, the heat, and I knew that when the weather changed we'd still be talking of the same thing, only then we'd be blowing at our hands and complaining of the cold.

That was the summer the garden walls seemed suddenly confining, when finally I was tall enough to peer over their mossy tops and look across the line of gardens and see sheets, dried out in the heat, listless in the still air, and hear the tinny music of distant transistor radios, and the ache of cars moving slowly in the hot sun, their windows wide as if that might change anything.

That was the summer they dug up Mr Mordecai's garden.

2 *Now use the grid to sum up the information you have underlined in ex. 1.*

Information – narrator	Quotes / Evidence from the text

3 *What is your first impression of the atmosphere? Read the text again very closely and mark the words and phrases which create this atmosphere. Now try to give a more detailed analysis of the setting at the beginning of this short story. Write down your ideas in the grid.*

Information – atmosphere	Quotes / Evidence from the text

4 *Why is the last line of the excerpt important? Make notes.*

Mediation: A news report

→S34
→pp. 26–27

When you want to help a speaker of German to understand an English text – written or spoken –, you must ask yourself if he or she needs to know every detail, or just the main points. In either case, the better you understand the text yourself, the better you can help.

TIP
Use the reading skills you know: reading for gist and for detail.

1 *Read this newspaper article about the surprising results of an official study.*

Police biased against young drivers

Which drivers get the most tickets for speeding? The teenagers, often in a hurry, always trying to impress their friends? That is what many people would guess – and that is what the insurance companies seem to believe. They charge young drivers higher insurance rates because, the companies claim, youngsters are less responsible and therefore a higher risk.

But a study carried out by the UK Department for Transport in 2008 does not come to this conclusion, at least, not as far as speeding is concerned. The study analyzed statistics on speeding and the age of the offenders during two periods: from 1997–1999 and from 2003–2005. In the earlier period the age group most likely to get tickets for speeding were the 24- to 34-year-olds. In the later period it was those aged between 45 and 59. Between these two periods, the number of men over 60 who received speeding tickets increased by 540 %. For women in this age group the figure went up by 1,200 %.

Does this mean that older people have lost their sense of responsibility and their respect for the law? Maybe, but there is also another explanation: – speed cameras, introduced to help the police to enforce speed limits on the roads. In 1997 there were less than 500 of these cameras in use; in 2005 there were about 5,000. They were installed to catch more offenders, and that is what they did. The total number of speeding tickets increased dramatically – especially for older drivers.

Before automatic cameras were introduced, speeding tickets were issued only by the police. When police officers catch someone speeding, they can decide whether to let the driver off with a warning or to issue a ticket. The statistics suggest that many police officers are biased against young drivers. An older driver is more likely to speed – but less likely to be ticketed by the police. But automatic cameras are not biased, they are blind. Everyone who gets caught gets a ticket.

2 *Answer the questions in German for someone who has difficulties in understanding the text.*

1. Um was geht es in der Studie?
2. Hat sich zwischen den beiden Zeiträumen in der Studie etwas geändert?
3. Wird ein bestimmter Grund dafür genannt?
4. Wieso spielt das eine Rolle? Was macht ein Polizist denn anders als eine Kamera?
5. Und wieso zeigt dieses Ergebnis, dass Polizisten voreingenommen sind?
6. Wie unfair! Hat das auch andere Folgen für junge Autofahrer?

Portfolio

Now it is time to think about what the exercises in Part A have shown you about your reading skills. What can you already do quite well? What aspects would you like to be better at? Go through the list and put an ✘ in the box which you think describes your level. Check to see if your teacher agrees with you, and use the exercises in Part B to help you improve the areas that need more practice.

How would you judge your skills in the following areas?	Already good	Must practise!	Exercises for extra practice: Part B
Skimming / Reading for gist			Page 20, ex. 1–2; page 21, ex. 1–2
Scanning / Reading for detail			Pages 22–23, ex. 1–3
Close reading			Pages 24–25, ex. 1–6
Mediation			Pages 26–27, ex. 1–2
Reading non-fictional texts			Page 20, ex. 1–2; page 21, ex. 1–2; pages 22–23, ex. 1–3
Reading fictional texts			Pages 24–25, ex. 1–6

Writing skills

→S23, S24
→pp. 30–31

TIP
First listen to the texts without writing down anything. Then listen again and take notes. Shorthand can help you to write faster, but don't try to write too much. Keywords and phrases will be enough to remind you of the facts you need.

Writing a factual text

When you write a factual text, you have to imagine that your reader knows nothing about the topic. Your text should have a clear, logical structure, and the information should be presented in good written style.

1 [◎] [▤] *Your task is to write a factual text about the history of carnival as background material for an exhibition of Caribbean culture in Britain. First collect information by listening to a radio programme about this topic. Listen for any important or interesting facts that are mentioned. Take notes on the four parts of the radio programme.*

2 *Look at your notes from ex. 1, decide which information you need and how you want to organize and structure your text. Use the grid below to make a plan showing the number of paragraphs and also the content summarized in one or two phrases. (There are different possibilities, and you might not need to use all the lines in the grid.) Don't forget to include a short introduction and conclusion.*

headdress a decorative covering for the head
Lent the 40 days before Easter in the Christian religion; a period in which some people stop doing particular things that they enjoy

Paragraph	Content

3 [👥] [▤] *Now write your text (2–4 sentences for each paragraph), using an appropriate style of language. When you have finished, first check your work yourself and then exchange texts with a partner. Help each other to find language mistakes (grammar, spelling, etc.) and also make helpful suggestions about what could be improved (text structure, content, style, etc.).*

TIP
Participle constructions can help to improve your written style.

4 *Think about what you had to correct or improve in your text and fill in the grid. You can use your checklist the next time you write a text.*

Grammar/Spelling	Choice of words	Style	Text structure

Writing a summary

→S20, S24
→pp. 32–33

Writing a summary means presenting the main ideas of a text in a much shorter form. As far as possible, you should use your own words, and you should not add any new ideas of your own.

1 *Before you write a summary you need to read and understand the text you are dealing with. First skim the newspaper article and in one sentence sum up the main point made by the writer.*

____

____

____

21st-century Britons are no longer either black or white

Andrew Kane, 28, an investment banker, his 26-year-old sister, Minna, a TV researcher, and friends who all described themselves as mixed-race, were having a drink in the pub and talking about the success of Lewis Hamilton and Barack Obama. "Everyone was saying, 'Here is the first black F1 champion, here is the first black American president,' and we thought, 'They are mixed-race,'" said Andrew. "We are not saying they should not be proud of their black heritage. But we are not just black and we are not just white."

The friends said they were fed up of being "bracketed" and decided to do something about it. They talked about setting up an organization "to celebrate mixed heritage" and within weeks the Turqoise Association was born.

The rise in mixed-race Britain is shown in a new report that shows young people are now six times as likely to be mixed-race as adults. The report paints a picture of Britain in which people of Caribbean, black African, Chinese, Indian and white British heritage are far more likely to fall in love, marry and have children with people of different races and the rate is increasing by the year. The majority of their mixed-race children will go on to enter relationships with people of yet another ethnic background.

Lucinda Platt, author of the report, said: "There has been a dramatic shift over 10 years. What we mean when we talk about minority groups is changing."

For Andrew and Minna, who have both Nigerian and white British heritage, it is all about identity. "In the past, a child of mixed race would ask their parents, 'What am I?'" said Andrew. "That was difficult for parents because identity was so tied to race. People felt forced into telling their children that they were 'black' or 'white' – it was a social conformity thing. But I would like to tell my children that they are mixed."

Brother and sister, who live in London, hope their group will help to promote discussion of mixed race. "We didn't feel mixed-race people, as an ethnic group, were reflected in the media," said Minna. "We wanted to show they are doing well and give younger mixed-race people role models. We celebrate the fact of being two cultures. It's like the best of both worlds."

Early research by the Turquoise Association found that the reason Caribbean men and women were most likely to enter mixed-race relationships was because they had been settled in Britain the longest. Platt agreed, and argued that other groups would move in the same direction the longer they stayed in Britain.

The dramatic change within some communities raises questions about the issues facing the children of mixed-race relationships in a society used to placing people into categories. As more and more people feel unable to identify with such groups, what future is there for them?

Some argue that it is largely about colour. Those who appear black or Asian are more likely to suffer discrimination than those who do not. That was the case for Elizabeth Biggs, 29, who grew up in Cheshire with her mother of Pakistani heritage and father who is white British. The fact that she appeared white means she did not suffer.

Others argued that the term "mixed-race" was divisive. Businessman Kenneth Olisa, whose parents are of different ethnic groups, said: "The faster people stop judging on things people cannot change and instead on things they can change, the faster we will achieve civilisation. I don't want to be called mixed-race, I want to be called Ken for my achievements."

The Observer, January 18, 2009

2 *Now read the article again more closely, underlining the main ideas and information and marking any new words or phrases you can't guess and which you think are important.*

3 [👥] *Check with a partner that you have both underlined the content you need for your summary. If you have marked different information, discuss whether it is necessary or not. Also try to help each other with any new words you find difficult. (If you really can't guess, use a dictionary.) Write down explanations on the right, expressing the same meaning in different words.*

TIP
Using different colours to underline different elements (content, new vocabulary, etc.) helps you to mark a text more clearly.

TIP
When you summarize what someone else has written, you should always mention the source.

4 [📄] *Make notes for a short summary. But don't just copy the text – as far as possible try to use your own words. Your English-English dictionary can help you to find similar words and expressions. Before you start, look again at all the ideas you have underlined. You might not need to include everything, especially if some ideas are repeated. You might also find that changing the order of some things can make your summary clearer.*

TIP
When you check your text, remember what you wrote down in ex. 4 on page 8!

5 [👥] [📄] *Turn your notes into a summary, writing short paragraphs that deal with different parts of the content. Think of a short introduction and conclusion. Check your work carefully, then ask a partner to look at it.*

→S19, S24
→p. 34

Writing an argumentative essay

An argumentative essay (also called a 'comment') discusses an issue about which people may disagree. You should present arguments for both sides, although you may also include your own opinion in the final part of the essay.

TIP
It is not important to agree as a group. Just express as many viewpoints as possible. This will help you to prepare for your essay.

1 [👥👥] *You are going to write a short essay discussing the statement: "A completely mixed-race population would make a better society than separate ethnic groups." First talk about this idea in groups, thinking about the effect a mixed-race population could have on issues like:*

integration • people's sense of identity • racial discrimination • how people are judged • local communities • individual cultures • ...

2 *Collect three or four arguments for and against the statement in ex. 1.*

For: ______________________________

____

____

____

Against: ______________________________

____

____

____

3 *Show that you understand the structure of an argumentative essay by writing down a few notes explaining what you should do in each part.*

Part	What you should do:
Introduction	
Main part	
Conclusion	

TIP
Think carefully whether you are for or against the statement. Ending with a strong argument can help to convince the reader.

4 [📄] *Write your argumentative essay. Follow the structure in ex. 3 and use your arguments from ex. 2 for the main part of your essay. Don't forget to check your work carefully. Be especially critical about whether you have managed to link your ideas and arguments smoothly.*

Creative writing

→S23, S24
→p. 35

The main rule in creative writing is that the form and style should match the type of text.

1 [👥] *Make a list of points you need to remember when you write the following kinds of text. The ideas in the box will help you to start thinking. When you have finished, compare your notes with a partner and add any important points you missed.*

- structure
- content
- perspective
- style of language
- type of vocabulary

1. **news report:** ______________________________

____

____

2. **diary:** ______________________________

____

____

3. **film scene:** ______________________________

____

____

4. **poem:** ______________________________

____

____

2 [👥👥] *First look at the three photos on your own and write a few notes about what you can see, how you think the people feel, what the background situation might be, etc. Then form groups of three or four and exchange your thoughts. Also say what ideas the photos give you for the different kinds of text in ex. 1. (Some text types might seem more suitable than others.)*

A

B

C

A: ______________________________

____

B: ______________________________

____

C: ______________________________

____

TIP
Write down everything that comes into your mind. There are no 'right' or 'wrong' ideas. Different people often see different things in the same picture.

TIP
- Collect ideas that belong together in the section.
- Mark your notes with different colours to show links, etc.
- A mind map can also help you to illustrate your ideas.

3 *Decide which of the text types in ex. 1 you want to write and which of the photos in ex. 2 you want to base it on. Then use the rest of the space in the box to collect ideas and words you might want to use in your text. Think of different aspects of the topic or situation you are writing about, and be as creative and imaginative as possible.*

Text type: ______________________ **Photo:** ______________

TIP
Think of a good beginning that will get the reader's attention right away e.g. a surprising statement, a strong image, a reference to a mysterious event.

4 *Work with your ideas from ex. 3. Choose which ones you want to use, and then plan and write your text in your exercise book. When you have finished, go back to your groups from ex. 2. Read each other's texts, correct mistakes and write down suggestions where you think the text must be improved.*

Portfolio

Now it is time to think about what the exercises in Part A have shown you about your writing skills. What can you already do quite well? What aspects would you like to be better at? Go through the list and put an ✘ *in the box which you think describes your level. Check to see if your teacher agrees with you, and use the exercises in Part B to help you improve the areas that need more practice.*

How would you judge your skills in the following areas?	Already good	Must practise!	Exercises for extra practice: Part B
Presenting factual information clearly and logically			Pages 30–31, ex. 1–5
Summarizing the content of a text			Pages 32–33, ex. 1–5
Writing an argumentative essay			Page 34, ex. 1–4
Thinking of ideas for creative writing			Page 35, ex. 1–4
Linking ideas and arguments smoothly			Page 36, ex. 1–3
Using participle constructions to improve written style			Page 37, ex. 1–3
Writing in the appropriate style for the type of text			Page 38, ex. 1–3
Expressing the same ideas in different words			Page 39, ex. 1–3
Using interesting and meaningful vocabulary			Page 40, ex. 1–4
Checking and improving written work			Page 41, ex. 1–2

Speaking skills

Giving a speech

→S28
→pp. 42–43

A good speech needs a clear structure and convincing content. It is also very important for the speaker to create a connection with the audience and to keep everyone listening.

1 *You are going to give a short speech about food waste as part of a campaign to help protect the environment. First study the following information and mark any facts and figures you think might be useful. (Not everything may be relevant.) Use a dictionary to look up any important new words.*

Reasons for throwing away food

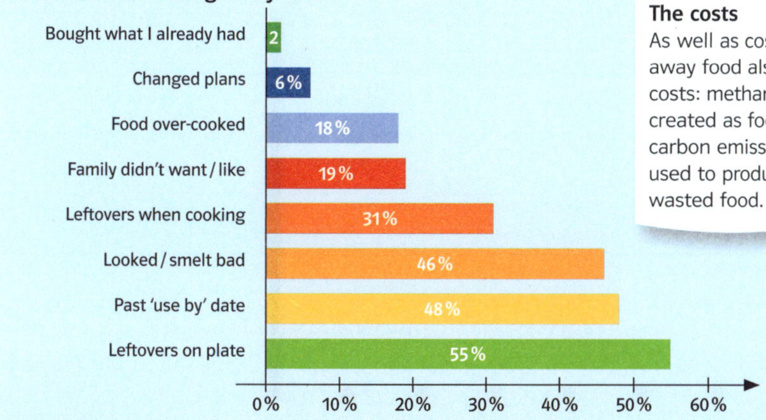

The costs
As well as costing money, throwing away food also has environmental costs: methane (a greenhouse gas created as food degrades) and the carbon emissions from the energy used to produce and transport wasted food.

FACT FILE

- There are two main types of food waste: inedible (peelings, bones, tea bags, etc.) and edible (food left on plate, 'out of date' food, etc.).
- On average, almost one third of all the food bought by households is wasted. Half of this is edible food.
- Food is more likely to be wasted by younger working people (aged 16–34) and families with school age children.

Food waste tips

REDUCE	• plan / store better • smaller portions
REUSE	• recipes for leftovers
RECYCLE	• compost • use food bin

FACT FILE

Where food waste goes

Ordinary bin:	73%
Food bin:	18%
Pets / wildlife:	18%
Compost:	14%

2 *Use the following grid to help you structure your speech. Write down what you are going to say in each part of the speech in order to give a clear, logical message about food waste. (You may not need to use all the lines in the grid.)*

Part	What you are going to say:
1	
2	
3	
4	

TIP
If you like, you can add your own information and ideas about food waste.

3 *Now prepare your speech, following the structure you developed in the grid in ex. 2. Use a separate note card for each part of your speech, think what you want to say and in what order, and make notes. Only write down keywords and phrases, facts and figures, etc. Don't write complete sentences.*

TIP
Remember that the beginning and end of a speech are especially important.

4 *Work in groups of three or four and give your speeches. Tell each other what you think is good or not so good. Think about the content and structure of the speech and also about the speaker's voice and body language. Write down your strong and weak points.*

→S11
→p. 44

Presenting film material

In a film presentation you should say what kind of film you are presenting, explain what the topic or main focus is, and comment on the audio-visual techniques that are used. You can also give your personal opinion on the film.

WORD BANK
expansion • fossil fuel • turbine • nuclear • to be conned • moor • threat • to blow

1 [🎬] *Work with a report which was filmed for the BBC TV programme 'Countryfile'. First look at the Word bank on the left. Watch the report once without writing down anything. Then watch it again and make notes on the aspects below. Don't try to remember all the details, just important points you might want to mention in a short presentation.*

Topic of report: ______________________

Scenes shown: ______________________

Facts reported: ______________________

____

Problems mentioned: ______________________

Background music: ______________________

2 [👥] [📄] *Compare the points you collected in ex. 1 with a partner. Then discuss how you would analyze and present this film. Think what you could say about: the topic, how the report is structured, how the spoken and visual information is linked, the effect of the music, etc. Prepare a short presentation (about 2 minutes) in note form. Each of you should have a copy of the notes.*

3 [👥] *Find a different partner and give your presentation. Also listen very carefully to what your new partner says about the film. Then go back to your first partner and tell him/her any good points you heard in the other presentation which you didn't include in yours.*

→S26
→p. 45

Taking part in an informal discussion

Taking part in a discussion means exchanging different points of view about an issue. At the same time you should be respectful towards other people who may have a different opinion.

TIP
Giving statistics can help you to make your point convincingly.

1 [👥👥] *Form groups of four or five and organize a role play discussion about the pros and cons of building many large wind farms to produce energy. At least two of you should support this idea and at least two should argue against it. Choose your roles and prepare for the discussion by identifying and marking the notes in the box that will help you to express arguments for your side.*

noise • clean source of energy • thousands of new jobs • thousands of turbines needed to produce energy for just one city • CO_2 emissions need to be cut by 80–90% by 2050 • wind speed always has to be over 10 mph • danger to birds and marine life • greatest need for energy in winter when winds usually strong • turbines easily damaged in thunderstorms • important to protect beautiful places • no pollution of land for future generations • even small wind farm with 20 turbines covers 1–2 sq. km • turbines generating 10% of all electricity needed would stand on only 0.02% of total land area • land under turbines can still be used for farming • can affect TV signals • endless renewable natural resource

2 [👥👥] *Act out your discussion, using the ideas you marked in ex. 1 and any other ideas you may have. Here are some points you should remember:*

- Help the discussion to develop naturally by reacting to what has just been said.
- If you want to introduce a new aspect, make this clear.
- Always be polite, even when you disagree strongly.
- Wait for the right moment to enter the discussion, and don't interrupt.

3 [👥👥] *Take a minute or two to comment on how successful you think your role play was. Was the tone appropriate for an informal discussion? Did the discussion develop smoothly? Were all the points and arguments relevant to the topic? Did anyone in the group talk too much or too little?*

Having a conversation

→S25
→p. 46

Conversations can be with people you already know or with complete strangers. Choosing a suitable topic, showing interest in what the other person says and also knowing what to say yourself – all these skills are part of developing a good conversation.

1 *Note down a few things you could mention or ask in a conversation with …*

1. these hikers you meet while you are walking in the hills:

____

____

____

2. these protesters you meet at a demonstration against climate change:

____

____

____

2 *What would be the first thing you would say to each of the people in ex. 1? Write down a suitable comment or question to start a conversation with …*

1. the hikers: ______________________________

2. the protesters: ______________________________

TIP
Your face, your body language and the tone of your voice can help you to look and sound friendly.

3 [👥] *Now work with a partner and develop the two conversations. In one conversation you should be yourself, and in the other conversation you should act the role of the person in the photo. Try to talk fluently for two or three minutes, and then think of a way to bring the conversation to an end.*

TIP
A good conversation partner listens and reacts to what the other person says.

Portfolio

Now it is time to think about what the exercises in Part A have shown you about your speaking skills. What can you already do quite well? What aspects would you like to be better at? Go through the list and put an ✘ *in the box which you think describes your level. Check to see if your teacher agrees with you, and use the extra exercises in Part B to help you improve the areas that need more practice.*

How would you judge your skills in the following areas?	Already good	Must practise!	Exercises for extra practice: Part B
Preparing and giving a speech			Pages 42–43, ex. 1–6
Analyzing and presenting film material			Page 44, ex. 1–4
Taking part in an informal discussion			Page 45, ex. 1–4
Developing a good conversation			Page 46, ex. 1–4
Speaking fluently and naturally			Page 47, ex. 1–3
Expressing oneself in an appropriate manner			Page 48, ex. 1–3
Making a point clearly and convincingly			Page 49, ex. 1–3
Expressing statistical information			Page 50, ex. 1–3
Interpreting diagrams			Page 51, ex. 1–3

Listening skills

→S29
→pp. 52–55

Listening for gist and for detail

You don't often have to listen to an unfamiliar text without having any information at all about what you are going to hear. When receiving a phone call, for example, you often recognize the caller's number before he or she speaks. When you check the Internet for what is on TV or the radio, you get the title of the programme and maybe some written information and a picture, too, before you listen to more information.

1 *You are going to listen to part of a speech given by the Australian Prime Minister Kevin Rudd on November 16, 2009. Before you listen, look at the heading and the photos and make notes about possible topics.*

It took a long time ...

____

____

2 [◎] *Listen to the speech. Don't write anything while you are listening at this stage. Concentrate on getting used to the speaker's voice and accent. Then sum up the gist of the text in just a few words. (Were any of your ideas in ex. 1 right?)*

____

____

3 [◎] *Now listen again for more detailed information. Write short answers to the following questions.*

1. Who is the Australian Prime Minister Kevin Rudd speaking to? ______________________________

____

____

2. What events is he apologizing for? (Give a few examples.) ______________________________

____

____

3. Where did these events take place? ______________________________

____

Then explain these quotes from the text.

1. "… austere and authoritarian places, where names were replaced by numbers."

___

___

2. "… as if this was not injury enough, you were left ill-prepared for life outside."

___

___

3. "[To] those of you separated on the dockside from your brothers and sisters; taken alone and unprotected to the most remote parts of a foreign land."

___

___

TIP Listen to the quotes again in the context of the whole text.

Taking notes while listening

→S30
→pp. 57–58

It is important to be able to make short notes quickly because otherwise you will miss the next part of the text while you are writing.

1 *You are going to listen to a radio interview in which a young woman tells a reporter about the voluntary work she does for an organization in her hometown. Write a list of the work you think she might do.*

___

___

2 [◎] *Listen to the interview. Were any of your ideas in ex. 1 right? Underline them while you are listening.*

3 [◎] *Now listen to the interview again. Make notes about the most important information while you are listening. If you can use any ideas from ex. 1 and 2, include them in your notes in the right place. Remember to use symbols and abbreviations.*

TIP Leave plenty of space between your notes so that you can add more.

What does she do?	Feelings?

4 [ÅÅ] *When you think your notes are complete, check with a partner. Then use your notes to give an oral summary of the interview to someone who has not heard it.*

→S32
→pp. 58–59

Guessing the meaning

Written texts: When you come across unfamiliar words in an English text, you can often guess their meaning. You already know different ways of doing this.

1 *Read the following text and try to understand as much as possible.*

In spite of heavy investment from the government and the voluntary sector, charities are still trying hard to recruit volunteers. According to government sources, volunteer numbers in England and Wales have declined since 2005.

New research by a youth volunteering body called "V" suggests the word 'volunteer' is part of the problem. Of the 2,000 young people surveyed in July, 66 % thought the term was scary. Some 21% said volunteering had a boring image, while 24% thought it was uncool.

The realization is spreading that the word volunteering does indeed have some negative connotations. Many organizations find they are better off simply asking people if they will help or join in. One "V" initiative will focus on the idea of doing someone a favour, rather than volunteering. But more than a facelift is needed.

The Guardian, September 10, 2008 (abridged)

2 *Guess the meaning of the underlined words and complete this chart with the German translation. Write down how you guessed (word family, similar German word, etc.).*

English	German	How did you guess?
investment		
have declined		
surveyed		
connotation		
do someone a favour		

Listening texts: When you come across unfamiliar words while listening to a text, it is often more difficult to guess the meaning of the words.

3 [◉] *You are going to listen to two excerpts from a news report about volunteering. Here are five words which you will hear (listed in chronological order). Try to guess what they mean from the context. Write down a German translation or an English paraphrase.*

English word	Meaning from the context
regimental	
providing / to provide	
mutually beneficial	
periphery	
power structure	

Mediation

→S34
→p. 60

1 [👥] [📋] *Look at the two photos. Why did the photographers take them? Is there a message? If so, does it come across well? Make notes and compare your ideas with a partner.*

2 [◎] *Grant is a young American who is well-informed about the problems which the homeless face in many parts of the USA. Listen to what he says to his friend Alison about it.*
Try to understand as much as possible.

TIP
Make sure that you understand the main ideas. Use the techniques you know to guess new words – written and spoken.

3 [◎] [📋] *A person who tries to help the homeless in Germany would like to know more about the situation in the USA. Listen to the conversation again and summarize the most important information in German. The ideas on the right can help you:*

FACT FILE
Although housing is a fundamental human right, homelessness is a problem in many developed countries, including the USA. According to a 2007 report, 3.5 million people become homeless – at least temporarily – each year.

Grundstückspreise und Imageschäden • Das Leben auf der Straße • Opfer von Verbrechen • Diskriminierung

Portfolio

Now it is time to think about what the exercises in Part A have shown you about your listening skills. What can you already do quite well? What aspects would you like to be better at? Go through the list and put an ✘ *in the box which you think describes your level. Check to see if your teacher agrees with you, and use the exercises in Part B to help you improve the areas that need more practice.*

How would you judge your skills in the following areas?	Already good	Must practise!	Exercises for extra practice: Part B
Listening for gist and for detail			Pages 52–54, ex. 1–4; pages 54–55, ex. 1–3; page 56, ex. 1–2
Taking notes while listening			Pages 57–58, ex. 1–4
Guessing the meaning			Pages 58–59, ex. 1–2
Mediation			Page 60, ex. 1–4
Understanding a news report			Pages 52–54, ex. 1–4
Understanding a radio interview			Pages 54–55, ex. 1–3
Understanding real conversations			Page 56, ex. 1–2
Understanding a speech			Pages 57–58, ex. 1–4

Reading skills

Skimming / Reading for gist: A research report →S1

1 Preparing to read

You are going to read part of a survey published by the Pew Research Center in the USA.

Look at the heading. Using the information you have so far, think what you might expect to read about in the text. Make notes here before you read.

____

____

____

A gentler generation gap

A | Earlier this summer the Pew Research Center conducted a new survey to probe more deeply into today's generation gap. Specifically, the survey asked whether or not young people and older people differ on certain core values or characteristics. In addition the survey attempted to find out whether these differences translated into conflicts between the generations – either in society at large, or at home between parents and children.

B | According to the survey, only one-in-ten parents with children ages 16 to 24 report they "often" had (or have) major disagreements with their children. In contrast, nearly twice as many adults (19 %) say that when they themselves were teenagers or in their early 20s, they often had serious arguments with their parents.

C | Of course, it is possible that parents are downplaying the seriousness of disagreements with their children or are offering a somewhat more dramatic version of their own childhood conflicts with their mothers and fathers. But an analysis of the survey findings among the different age groups taking part shows that, broadly speaking, parents' and children's accounts of intrafamily quarreling were consistent.

D | Among parents with children ages 16 to 24, slightly fewer than half (45 %) say they have major disagreements "often" or "sometimes". When respondents ages 16 to 24 were asked a complementary question about disagreements with their parents, an almost identical proportion (42 %) report they often or sometimes have serious arguments with their parents.

E | In addition to arguing less, parents report spending more time with their younger children than their parents spent with them – and the proportion who express this view appears to have increased in recent years. Nearly half (48 %) of all parents with children 16 or younger say they are spending more time with their children than their parents spent with them, up from 42 % in a survey conducted for Newsweek magazine in 1993.

F | Whether accurate reflections of family life or self-serving versions of history, these findings together with other survey results suggest that conflicts between the generations appear to have eased considerably in recent decades – both in the home and in society at large.

2 Skimming / Reading for gist

a) *Read the whole text once. Tick the statement that sums up the gist of the text best.*

1. There are no longer any serious conflicts between the generations. ☐
2. Arguments between the generations are increasing, but there is not so much physical violence. ☐
3. Today there is more contact and less conflict between the generations than in the past. ☐
4. Parents and their children argue less than in the past because they spend less time together. ☐

b) *Match each of these sentences with a paragraph in the text.*

- Today's parents say they spend more time with their young children than their own parents spent with them. ☐
- Even allowing for untruthful evidence, the general results about arguments seem to be reliable. ☐
- The relationship between the generations seems to have improved generally. ☐
- The question is: Do different generations have different values which are a source of conflict? ☐
- Parents' reports about arguments match what their young adult children say. ☐
- Today's adults experience less conflict with their children than with their own parents in the past. ☐

Skimming / Reading for gist: A teen website →S1

1 Finding out the basic similarities and differences

a) *These three texts are all from the same article / source. Read them all once. Write down what they have in common.*

A Two of the main reasons people are bullied are because of appearance and social status. Bullies pick on the people they think don't fit in, maybe because of how they look, how they act, their race or religion, or because the bullies think their target may be gay or lesbian.

Some bullies attack their targets physically, which can mean anything from pushing to hitting, or even sexual assault. Others use psychological control or verbal insults as instruments of power. For example, people in popular groups or cliques often bully people they categorize as different by excluding them or gossiping about them (psychological bullying). They may also tease their targets (verbal bullying). Verbal bullying can also involve sending cruel instant or e-mail messages or even posting rude comments about a person on a website – practices that are known as cyberbullying.

B Ignore the bully and walk away. It's definitely not a coward's response – sometimes it can be harder than losing your temper. Bullies depend on the reaction they get, and if you walk away, or ignore hurtful e-mails or instant messages, you're telling the bully that you just don't care. Sooner or later the bully will probably get bored with trying to bother you. Walk tall and hold your head high. Using this type of body language sends a message that you're not vulnerable.

Hold the anger. Who doesn't want to get really upset with a bully? But that's exactly the response he or she is trying to get. Bullies want to know they have control over your emotions. If you're in a situation where you have to deal with a bully and you can't walk away with dignity, use humor – it can throw the bully off guard. Work out your anger in another way, such as through exercise or writing it down (make sure you tear up any letters or notes you write in anger).

C All of us have to deal with a lot of difficult situations. For some people, when they're feeling stressed, angry, or frustrated, hurting someone else can be a quick escape – it takes the attention away from them and their problems. Some bullies learn from firsthand experience. Perhaps name-calling, putdowns, or physical force are the norms in their families. Whatever the reason, though, it's no excuse for being the bully.

If you find it hard to resist the temptation to bully, you might want to talk with someone you look up to. Try to think about how others feel when you tease or hurt them. If you have trouble figuring this out (many people who bully do), you might ask someone else to help you think of the other person's side.

Bullying behavior backfires and makes everyone feel unhappy – even the bullies. People might feel intimidated by bullies, but they don't respect them. If you would rather that people see your strength and character – even look up to you as a leader – find a way to use your power for something positive rather than to put others down.

b) [▤] *Make a grid like the following and sum up the gist of each text, pointing out the main differences between them.*

Text	Main gist

2 Looking for keywords

a) *Read each text separately and underline words and phrases which seem especially important for that aspect of bullying.*

TIP
Particularly important words and phrases are often repeated, or they are explained through examples.

b) [▤] *Look again at the words and phrases you have underlined. Make a grid like the following. Then write down 4–8 keywords for each text.*

Text	Keywords

Scanning / Reading for specific information →S1

1 An official website

a) *This UK government website gives tips and information about using the Internet. You are looking for information about buying things online. Before you scan this text, make a list of keywords to look for.*

____

____

TIP
Don't try to look for too many keywords at once. It's often quicker to concentrate on one keyword at a time.

b) *Read the text and underline words and phrases which go with your keywords.*

Staying safe online

Some websites will ask you to fill out a registration form before you can use them. While this is normal, it is a good idea to find out what the website will do with your personal details.
All companies that collect information have to tell their customers how personal information will be used. Make sure you check the website's terms and conditions if you want to know.
Some sites allow other companies to use details from their user database for market research purposes. Companies have to give you the chance to tell them if you don't want your details to be used in this way. This is often done by having a tick box on the online registration page. If you don't want your information to be used, tick that box before you submit your information.
Many people still don't like shopping on the Internet because they think their bank details are not safe. Luckily, shopping on the web is now just as safe as ordering goods over the telephone, as long as you follow a few common sense rules. If you do order goods over the Internet, make sure that the company you're buying from uses a secure shopping server. You'll know if it is a secure site if a padlock icon appears at the bottom of your browser window, or the web address begins with 'https:'.
If it's a company that you've never heard of before, search their site for any contact numbers and postal addresses. If they're a respectable company, they won't mind you giving them a quick call to ask them a few questions.
Also, make sure that you never send your bank details to anyone in an e-mail. Banks and online stores will never ask you to do this as it is not a secure way of sending information.
If you do receive an official-looking e-mail that asks you to send your financial details, you should never reply as you could become a victim of identity fraud.

2 An advert

[⊡] *A Rihanna fan has heard about the 'Gold Circle' tickets for the concert in Nottingham. Read this ad and underline the information about how much these tickets cost and what they offer.*

RIHANNA LIVE IN NOTTINGHAM!

Get ready to experience a night of superstar entertainment when Rihanna plays at Trent FM Arena Nottingham this Friday. Rihanna will be wowing audiences with tracks from her new studio album, 'Rated R', plus massive hits like 'Umbrella' from previous albums.

- General tickets are on sale now priced at £39.50 and £45 (plus booking fee).
- For an extra special treat, why not check out our Gold Circle Packages! The Gold Circle is an exclusive cordoned off standing area directly in front of the stage, giving you the best experience of this groundbreaking show from one of the world's biggest superstars. And not only will you have the best view in the house you will also meet Rihanna! This package also includes access to the VIP room, snacks and drinks, a T-shirt and a tour laminate.
- Gold Circle – £150 (booking fee when paying by card £15 per ticket).
- Gold Circle Meet and Greet – £300 (booking fee when paying by card £17.50 per ticket).
- Details of when and where to arrive for the meet and greet will be emailed to you about 10 days prior to the show.
- To purchase your tickets and to find out more information, you can call our 24hr ticket hotline on 08444 124 624 or go on-line at www.trentfmarena.com.

3 A newspaper report

a) *Before you read the text, look at the photo and read the headline. Write down what you think the gist of the text will be.*

b) *Now read the text for gist. Check what you wrote in a) and change it if necessary.*

Many teen mums are just lonely

There are so many young mothers on the Gleadless Valley Estate in Sheffield that it is known locally as "Push Chair Alley".

These teenage girls that I'm talking to (their names have been changed) are still very much children. They are taking part in a sexual health project on the estate – one of the poorest neighbourhoods in Sheffield, and one with a high level of teenage pregnancy.

"If people's lives are rubbish they just think a baby is going to make it better," says Jackie. But with her mouth full of sweets she is difficult to understand.

"If their Mums and Dads don't care about them they think 'I won't be lonely any more if I have a baby'," says another girl, looking through her bag for a second toffee.

"They feel more grown up if they are responsible over something, if they have to take care of something (a child) instead of being taken care of," she adds.

It is as if caring for a child – something few at this age are well equipped to do – will suddenly turn them into adults.

The trained nurse who organizes the meetings, Julie Norburn, has an easy, relaxed relationship with the girls. She puts a lot of teenage pregnancies locally down to alcohol and drugs.

"They are in situations where they are having sex and they are not in control," she says.

And that often results in risky behaviour, often caused by peer pressure, or in some cases because they "just want to have some love from someone".

Martin, who is 17, is "scared". He learned recently that his girlfriend – who is younger than him – is pregnant, but what he feared most was telling his mum. He is desperately trying to do the right thing and, unlike many people on the estate, he has got a job. But he has been in trouble with the police before and he is not exactly welcomed by his girlfriend's parents.

But although he seems shocked and sad, he says teenage pregnancy is "normal" here. People "get used to it", he adds, and because it is so common, in a way "no one is bothered". Martin has not seen his girlfriend for a while, but he says he is saving up for the baby. His girlfriend will live with her mother at first, but they have got their name down for council housing. But Martin knows that could take years.

In the end teenage pregnancy is not about statistics but the real lives of young and vulnerable people. In effect they are child parents, ill equipped to deal with the challenges of their own lives – let alone the demands of raising another generation.

BBC News, January 12, 2009 (abridged)

c) *Scan the text for information about the social and economic situation of the people on the Gleadless Valley Estate. Underline the phrases in the text, then write a short summary in note form.*

d) *Quote the parts of the text which tell you …*

a) that some girls hope a baby will give them the love they don't get from their parents.	
b) that they seem to think that being responsible for a child will suddenly make them mature.	
c) that some girls get pregnant because of the influence of other teenagers.	
d) that teenage pregnancy is not considered unusual in this area.	

Reading a fictional text (close reading) →S1

1 Preparing to read a fictional text

Look at the heading and the outer form of this text. What do you expect the text to be about?

TIP
Look at the length of the paragraphs, the punctuation, etc.

2 Reading for gist

[👥] *Read the whole text without looking anything up. Concentrate on the characters and the action. Sum up the events in one or two sentences. Then check with your partner.*

TIP
Remember the key questions: Who? Where? When? What happens?

Just Along for the Ride by Dennis Kurumada

I leaned back on the seat and watched the back of Dick's head as he steered. The '55 DeSoto rumbled along the rain-soaked street.

This evening's gonna be a total loss, I thought. Things have gotta be pretty dull when all you've got to do is drive around with a friend who just got his license. But it beats sitting at home. So there we were, five of us. Dick and Phil were in front. Reid, Steve, and I were in the back. We were all cold, damp, and bored. Man, we needed something to do!

"This is really crummy. I think we …"

I was cut off by Phil. "Hey, let's drive up to somebody … some kid … and flatten him."

"What?" I said.

"We drive up slow, then swing open the door real fast, and knock the guy on his can."

We all looked at him kinda funny.

"Well, it's something to do," Phil said.

"Aw, why not? Okay, we'll do it."

We began looking around for a victim.

"You guys are nuts," I said. "What if he calls the cops?"

"You worry too much. Whenever we wanna have some fun, you always chicken out."

"There's one!"

It was raining hard, but we could see the blurred figure of some guy under a streetlight on the corner. Steve laughed.

"Oh wow! This is gonna be funny."

A couple of us started laughing.

"Will you guys shut up?" said Dick. I guess it made him nervous.

The kid was about half a block away. The street wasn't too busy. Only a few cars were around. Dick started weaving across the road.

"Stop fooling around!" I said.

Steve got on the door, ready to open it. Then everything started happening too fast. The guy at the corner stepped out into the street. The car swerved. The door swung open, and Steve started falling out.

He grabbed my arm, and we both fell back on the seat. Dick got scared and threw the car away from the kid.

The headlights flashed on a frozen figure. I could see his face, eyes wide, mouth open. There was a squeal of tires on the slick street and a hollow thud as the figure was hurled, rolling across the roof. I got all mixed up.

"Ken Benjamin!" I said. "I think that was Ken Benjamin!"

Dick slowed down. Then he suddenly started speeding down the street.

"Dick! Stop! I know that guy! Dick, will ya stop?" He didn't hear me. "Stop the car! He's my friend!"

I hit him on the shoulder and grabbed his shirt. He turned around. Tears were blobbing up in his eyes.

"Shut up, you jerk! You want us to get nailed for man-slaughter?" He hit my arm.

What a stupid thing to do! I got so scared that I started shivering like crazy. I just couldn't believe it. I felt sick. (…)

It was 12:30 when I got home. Nobody was awake. I started pacing around the kitchen. I was so scared. I didn't know if we had killed him or not. I turned on the radio and listened to some music. But when the news came on, I turned it off. You idiot, I thought. Ken was your friend. Go to his mom or something. Well, I didn't hit him! It's not my fault! Those other guys … it wasn't my idea … no! You were in the car. You're responsible, too. Hit and run, hit and run.

I got in my car and drove for a while. Then I started remembering things Ken used to say.

"I don't know what to do!" I was shouting as I drove. No answer. My mind burned. "Go see Mrs. Benjamin, you coward!"

But I couldn't. I just couldn't. When I got home, the lights were on. My mother was in her robe.

"Your friends are here," she said. "I don't think that two o'clock in the morning is the right time to …"

I didn't listen. I just went into the front room. Dick walked up to me and said real low, "I heard on the radio that he's not dead. He isn't even hurt bad."

I didn't say anything. I just looked at him.

"No one knows," he went on. "So maybe we can get away with it."

He could see I was getting mad. I could have killed him.

The others stood up and came over. I didn't say a thing. I just walked out the door, got in the car, and left.

It took me a while to find Ken's house. It was gray brick, and the lights were on. Maybe it wasn't gray. I don't know. Everything looked gray. I walked up and rang the doorbell.

3 Identifying different parts of the text

Read the text again and divide it up into 4–6 sections. Mark them A, B, C, D, … and find a short heading or summary for each of them.

A ____________________ D ____________________

B ____________________ E ____________________

C ____________________ F ____________________

4 Finding out about the external structure of the plot

Make a grid like the following. Then write down as much information as possible about where and when the action takes place.

Lines	Place	Time

5 Analyzing the narrator's attitude

Find the parts of the text which give you the following information:

TIP
Underline the phrases in the text first, then write down the line numbers together with the beginning and end of the quotes.

	Lines	Quote
plan is crazy – it might mean trouble		
against driving away – injured victim is friend		
fear affects him physically		
in his mind – tries to deny responsibility		
realizes he is guilty, too		
knows he should face up to consequences but can't		
decides to break with friends and act		

6 Looking for more details

a) *Read the first part of the story (up to line 29). Underline phrases which contribute to the atmosphere of the situation, then sum it up in your own words.*

____

b) *Find more phrases and sentences which show the narrator's conflict about his responsibility. Underline them with a different colour.*

Mediation → S34

1 Understanding a news report

a) [👥] *The headline of this article could be translated as "Sportstars nicht mehr so wichtig als Vorbilder". With a partner discuss what information you might expect to find. Then read the text.*

Sports stars fading as role models

The US National Football League recently penalized a star player for off-the-field behavior not befitting the "higher standards" the league expects from its players. One of the factors behind higher standards for athletes is the perception that professional athletes serve as role models for admirers, especially children and teens. However, this perception may not be accurate. A new UK study finds the loutish and drunken behavior of some of our sporting heroes has little or no effect on the drinking habits of young people.

University researchers in the UK and in Australia, say their findings – published in Drug and Alcohol Review – contradict the idea that sports stars act as role models for those who follow sports.

"Our research shows that young people, both sportspeople and non-sportspeople, don't appear to be influenced by the drinking habits of high-profile sportspeople as portrayed in the mass media," said lead researcher Dr. Kerry O'Brien, a lecturer in Manchester's School of Psychological Sciences.

Dr. O'Brien and his colleagues, pointing to previous research, suggest that sports stars are much more likely to influence the drinking behavior of fans when used as marketing tools by the alcohol industry for marketing campaigns, such as through sponsorship deals.

The research team asked more than 1,000 young sportspeople at elite and amateur level and non-sportspeople to state what they thought the drinking behavior of high-profile sport stars was, compared with their friends. They were then asked to report their own drinking behaviour.

The researchers found that both sporting and non-sporting taking part in the study believed that sports

stars actually drank significantly less than themselves, but that their own friends drank much more.

Sports stars' drinking was not related to young sportspeople's own drinking – but it was related to lower levels of drinking in non-sportspeople. – The more alcohol non-sportspeople believed sports stars to drink, the less they actually drank themselves.

Dr. O'Brien added: "Sport administrators, like the UK Football Association, are very quick to criticize and punish individual sport stars for acting as poor role models when they are caught behaving drunkenly. But there is much stronger evidence for a relationship between alcohol-industry sponsorship, advertising and marketing within sport and dangerous drinking among young people than there is for the influence of sports stars drinking.

"Of course sports stars should drink responsibly, but it's dishonest to place the blame on them for setting the bad example. It is time that sport administrators think about their own social responsibilities when weighing up the costs and advantages of using their sports and sport stars to market alcohol for the alcohol industry."

b) [✍] *Which of these topics are mentioned in the text? Tick the right boxes.*

1. Teilnehmer der Studie sollten verschiedene Trinkgewohnheiten vergleichen. ☐
2. Die Trinkgewohnheiten prominenter Sportler haben wenig Einfluss auf Andere. ☐
3. Gewalt beim Sport geht auf das negative Vorbild von Sportstars zurück. ☐
4. Es gab unterschiedliche Ergebnisse für männliche und weibliche Teilnehmer der Studie. ☐
5. Die These, dass Spitzensportler als Vorbilder dienen, wird revidiert. ☐
6. Alkohol in der Sportwerbung hat einen größeren Einfluss als das Verhalten prominenter Sportler. ☐
7. Die Studie wurde in zwei Ländern durchgeführt. ☐
8. Die Trinkgewohnheiten von Jugendlichen haben sich gewandelt. ☐

c) [✍] [▤] *Summarize the contents of the article in German, using the following topics:*

- Die Rolle von Spitzensportlern als Vorbilder für Jugendliche
- Der Verlauf der Studie und ihre Ergebnisse
- Gefährliche Einflüsse auf den Alkoholkonsum von Jugendlichen

2 Reading a book review

A good review helps the reader to decide whether he / she would like to read the book, see the movie or play the game. It contains information about the contents and also gives the reviewer's opinion about the quality. This opinion is usually supported by examples from the work, e. g. quotations.

The Absolutely True Diary of a Part-Time Indian by Sherman Alexie

The title tells it like it is. Sherman Alexie was born a Spokane Indian. He grew up where the book is set, on a reservation – the "rez" – in Wellpinit, Washington state. He was, like his central character, born with a brain illness. And in his teens he attended Reardan High School, off the reservation, near the rich farm town, where all the other students were white.

Arnold Spirit Jr, known simply as Junior on the rez, speaks directly to the reader and is both narrator and illustrator, a cartoonist. He feels like rubbish, gets beaten up as a matter of course because he lisps, stutters and looks like a freak, but with a pen in his hand he finds a sense of being "important". He can at least express what it's like living his life. He needs just a couple of words to describe his parents. – She is an ex-drunk. He is a drunk. In fact Junior only knows five Indians who have never drunk alcohol, one of them being his bandana-wearing grandmother: "Drinking would shut down my seeing and my hearing and my feeling."

Junior might have brain damage but he is following in grandmother's footsteps, engaged with the world, full of anger and energy. Too full. When he sees his mother's name in a geometry textbook in class, he just cannot accept that his generation are still studying from the same books as the last. There is a graphic illustration of a boy throwing a book at his white teacher and breaking his nose. Suspension follows.

But then the injured teacher comes to visit. He isn't happy about Junior's assault but he's also full of guilt, as his job has been to educate their culture out of his Indian students. And he has some advice for Junior: "You have to take your hope and go somewhere where other people have hope." And the most hope belongs to white people. So Junior makes the brave decision to leave his home and go to Reardan. No matter that he has to walk more than 20 miles to get there each day because there isn't enough money for gas.

He finds friendship with a geek, Rowdy, who teaches him the art of reading. He gets to be the semi-boyfriend of the beautiful, milky Penelope. Even the sports guys learn to respect him, especially when he turns out to be a whizz on the basketball court. The only problem is that there are regular on-court battles against the team from his old school, whose star player used to be his best friend, who sees him as a traitor. And so he must be brave enough to face his people and defeat them. In his own words, this is "really weird".

Some books are like living organisms. They seem to breathe, laugh, cry, joke, challenge, meet you eye to eye. Maybe it's the combination of drawings, funny comments, truth, tragedy, despair and hope that makes this more than an entertaining read, more than an engaging story about a North American Indian kid who makes it out of a poor, dead-end background without losing his connection with who he is and where he's from.

Opening this book is like meeting a friend you'd never make in your actual life and being given a piece of his world, inner and outer. It's humane, authentic and, most of all, it speaks.

a) *What can you tell a German friend who is thinking of reading the book? Answer his / her questions briefly.*

1. Wer ist Arnold Spirit Jr. und was passiert mit ihm?
2. Wieso ist im Titel von einem *Part-Time Indian* die Rede?
3. Was erfährt man über den Autor, Sherman Alexie?
4. Was findet die Kritikerin so gut an dem Buch?

b) *Your friend thinks the book sounds rather depressing. Tell him (in German) about two episodes in the story in which Junior makes a positive step forwards.*

Emphatic forms →G1

Emphatic forms are used to stress the important words or phrases in what is written or said. In spoken language emphasis can be given through intonation. In written texts it must be done with the choice of words and the word order.

1 Recognizing emphatic forms

a) *Read what this boy wrote in a teenage blog and underline the emphatic forms.*

It's really hard being a teenager today. The pressure from other teens and from the media is bad enough, but it's the older generation who give us the most trouble. Adults go on about "wild, irresponsible young people" – as if they themselves had never done anything crazy in their youth! Take my parents, for example. They're forever criticizing the way I spend my time. They say I go out too often and neglect my schoolwork completely. But in fact I do take an interest in school and I'm terribly disappointed myself when my grades aren't too good. My parents don't like my best friend. That's OK with me, but what I hate is the way they say, "You're the one who must make the decisions – but we do feel you should avoid people like Susan." Don't get me wrong. I'm not one of those kids who's always fighting with her parents. We don't argue all the time, and their opinion of some things does matter to me. But my parents will never choose my friends. That's absolutely out of the question!

b) [👥] *Compare your results with a partner. What different types of emphasis can you identify together?*

___

___

2 Using emphatic forms

Write the second part of these mini-dialogues. Use the notes and an emphatic form.

1. "Why didn't you phone me yesterday?" – (phone • no answer)

___

2. "Rick and I split up, but somehow I can't forget him." – (need • new circle • friends)

___

3. "Janice is taking part in the skating championships next week." – (but • Janice • say skating • waste of time)

___

4. "Why don't you want to sit next to Michelle?" – (always • talk about • rich friends)

___

5. "Would you like me to help you with your bike?" – (no • I • repair)

___

6. "You shouldn't drink so much alcohol." – (I • drink • own business)

___

Using adverbs and adverbials →G3

By using adverbs and adverbials you make your texts more detailed and precise. You can add more emphasis and colour with adverbs and adverbials, too.

1 Identifying different types of adverbs and adverbials

Read the text below. Underline the adverbs and adverbials, using a different colour for each type. (Make a key to the exercise by underlining these categories in your chosen colours, too.)

TIP
You can check up on types of adverbs and adverbials in G3b).

time • place • manner • frequency • comment

Treena first heard about drugs from Lisa, who lived nearby. It was soon after Treena's thirteenth birthday. The two girls weren't real friends, but they occasionally walked their dogs in the park together. One day Lisa said to Treena in a low voice, "I'm into drugs, you know." Then she walked away without another word. Treena was shocked, of course, but at the same time she was secretly fascinated. Next time she saw Lisa, she said to her as casually as she could, "Quite frankly, Lisa, I'm sure you've never taken drugs. – You just wanted to impress me that day in the park."

2 Practising word order with adverbs and adverbials

Write these sentence parts in a suitable order. Add punctuation marks where necessary. (There is often more than one possibility.)

TIP
Number the parts of each sentence in the right order before you start to write.

1. frequently • from teenagers who are • clearly • with peer pressure • agony aunt Lauren • unable to deal • receives e-mails
2. many parents • when their child is • under the influence • especially at school • of other teenagers • don't always notice • gradually falling • unfortunately
3. One girl wrote: • trying to get me • in my class • interested in drugs • are constantly • some kids
4. people • get involved • because they want to belong • in their neighborhood • during their teenage years • accidentally • to an influential group • in negative activities • sometimes
5. Lauren points out: • it's a question • without trying • who let you decide • to influence you • the right friends • of choosing • freely • basically

3 Improving your style with adverbs and adjectives

a) *Mark or underline the places in the text where you want to add an adverb or adjective – or to replace one that is there already. Make a list of your improvements and additions.*

Here are two examples: 1 Last weekend 2 from Bristol

TIP
You can use adverbs, adverbials and adjectives to improve the style of this newspaper report. They can make the language more precise – and also more colourful.

1 A teenage boy 2 became the hero of the hour when he fought flames to rescue five children from their home.

Neighbour Leighton Griffiths, 15, saved the children aged between four and 15 when their house went up in flames early on Saturday morning. Eye-witnesses said the children, who were in the house alone, were screaming as smoke came out of the windows.

Then Leighton, with help from his stepfather, kicked the back door in, but was forced back by the smoke at 2.20 am. Leighton then made his way round the front of the house, picked up a hosepipe connected to the water supply and fought his way through the flames.

Once inside, Leighton helped three of the children get out of the window, with the help of his stepfather who had fetched a ladder. Another neighbour helped to put out the flames from outside with the hosepipe, while Leighton carried the other two children out of the house through the front door.

After he had rescued all the children, Leighton, who is asthmatic, collapsed and was taken to hospital where he was treated for smoke inhalation, burns and a suspected broken rib.

In spite of the good job he had done, the teenager remained calm about his achievement. "I just acted on instinct," he said.

b) *Write your improved text. Then compare it with your partner's.*

Writing skills

How to write a factual text →S23, S24

1 Analyze a text about reggae music

a) *Read the information about reggae and divide the text into three paragraphs. Show where each paragraph begins by underlining the first word in red. Then write down the main focus of each paragraph.*

Paragraph 1: ______________________________

Paragraph 2: ______________________________

Paragraph 3: ______________________________

Reggae around the world

Although almost everyone is familiar with reggae music, most people do not know much about its origins. Starting in Jamaica in the late 1960s, reggae grew out of two other local music styles, ska and rock steady. Ska had a fast, strong sound, characterized by its typically African rhythm, while rock steady songs were slower and had lyrics about everyday life and social problems. Reggae used the rhythm of ska but slowed it down a little, and also used the lyrics to give a message. It is thought that the first reggae record was "Do the Reggay" by Toots and the Maytals in 1968, and that the name 'reggae' came from a dance style. Having become popular in Jamaica very quickly, reggae soon began to spread across the world. First this new kind of music was introduced to an international audience by singers like Jimmy Cliff and Peter Tosh. Then Bob Marley, the most famous reggae star of them all appeared. In spite of his early death from cancer in 1981, Marley became a worldwide superstar. In many people's eyes he was mainly responsible for turning reggae into an important music genre, which would survive over the years and also help to create new styles of music, like dub, hip-hop and rap. Today, reggae can still be heard around the world, sung and enjoyed by people who were not even born when it first began. Like other music styles, it has continued to grow and develop so that now there are many bands playing different forms of reggae. The basic character and elements are still at the heart of the music, however, and old-style reggae will always be popular with true fans.

b) [👥] *Check with a partner to see if you agree about your ideas in a). Then work together to identify and mark good style elements in the text: time adverbials that help to structure the content, conjunctions that help to link ideas smoothly, participle constructions that make the style more fluent, etc. Use different colours for these elements.*

2 Find out about Bhangra music

a) [👥] *Look at the two photos. What is similar / different? Talk about it with your partner.*

b) *Read what Bhangra fans say about their favourite music.*

- The name? It comes from an old Punjabi dance.
- It gives young Asians everywhere – well, a sense of identity, a link to their own culture, all that kind of thing.
- Bhangra arrived in the UK in the 1960s. With the Asian immigrants, of course.
- Now it's a global industry. Yes, definitely big business.
- Believe it or not, Bhangra goes back to the 14th century.
- It was young British Asians who began to develop the modern style – oh, back in the 1970s.
- Sure, today there are new forms, but it's still all Bhangra.
- They use a drum called a 'dhol' – that's what gives the music its fantastic rhythm and energy.
- British-style Bhangra – well, you could say it started a similar trend with Asians in other countries.
- It's part of the culture of Punjab – that's a region in north-west India and Pakistan.
- These days all the kids love Bhangra – I mean, not just Asians. It's such great dance music.
- Mixing traditional Bhangra with hip-hop and other western music – wow, that created an amazing new sound!

3 Plan your text

a) *Make a plan for a factual text about Bhangra music. Follow the three-paragraph structure of the text about reggae. Write down the topic of each paragraph and use the information in ex. 2 to note down keywords about the content.*

Paragraph 1 Topic: ____________________

Content: ____________________

Paragraph 2 Topic: ____________________

Content: ____________________

Paragraph 3 Topic: ____________________

Content: ____________________

b) [⏎] [▤] *Your text should be in good written style instead of the informal spoken style in ex. 2. Practise this in your answers to the following questions. Write full sentences.* →p. 38

1. Where does Bhangra music originally come from?
2. How is the typical rhythm and energy of Bhangra created?
3. How was Bhangra introduced to the UK?
4. In what way is modern Bhangra different from the traditional style?
5. What is the importance of Bhangra to young Asians around the world?
6. Why has Bhangra become popular with young people of all ethnic groups?

4 Write your text →pp. 36–37

[▤] *Go through your plan in ex. 3a) critically, making any changes in content or order you think necessary. Then write your text, trying to achieve a smooth, fluent style. Use the checklists on page 41 to help you check and improve your work.*

TIP

Look again at how the information about reggae was expressed in ex. 1. Maybe you can use some of the same sentence constructions or linking elements.

5 Further practice

[⏎] [▤] *Write another text about a different kind of music you are interested in. Do your own research, make a plan showing the structure and content, and then write your text.*

How to summarize a text →S20, S24

1 Read and understand the text

a) *First read the article for the gist. Match the headings to the six paragraphs and complete the grid with the right letters.*

Paragraph	1	2	3	4	5	6
Heading						

A: Multi-ethnic dialect replaces cockney • B: Spoken in London and other cities • C: Not allowed in the classroom
D: Teens speak new multi-ethnic dialect • E: Spread by music • F: Speakers from all backgrounds

It's a new black-white language

Linguists have identified Britain's first multi-ethnic dialect – a variant of English that includes words and sounds from cockney, Jamaican creole, Bengali and other languages. The dialect is becoming the standard way for teenagers of different ethnic groups to communicate across the racial divide. While it may be baffling to teachers and parents, researchers believe it will spread and become a part of everyday English over the next 20 years.

Professor Paul Kerswill, who led the study, said: "Inner-city Londoners are using a new kind of English as their everyday speech." Kerswill said similar ways of speaking were emerging in multicultural cities such as Birmingham, Bristol and Manchester. "We think this multi-ethnic kind of speech will become more mainstream through force of numbers with migration, and because it is fashionable and cool."

The spread of the dialect is being encouraged by a wave of successful London rap stars such as Lady Sovereign and Dizzee Rascal. G Money, a DJ at 1Xtra, the BBC youth radio station, said: "Music is responsible for its spread, especially with stations like 1Xtra playing it on a national basis instead of the local pirate stations. I was in Watford the other day, but the kids on the street corner were no different from the kids that hang around in London. They all dress the same and speak the same – isn't that a beautiful thing?"

Kerswill's team first identified the dialect at an inner-city college in Hackney, east London, during a research programme into teenage English. The study involved analyzing the conversation of 32 teenagers aged 16 to 18. Half were from white British backgrounds and half from immigrant families. The team found all the students used the same multi-ethnic dialect, regardless of their background.

The accent was peppered with different influences. The word "face", for example, was pronounced as the longer "feeece", which researchers believe is West Indian in origin. When saying "pound" the students reverted to the cockney pronunciation of "paaand". The vocabulary included words originating from the Indian subcontinent such as "nang", meaning good, and "creps" for trainers, a word which probably comes from Jamaica. The multi-ethnic dialect is replacing traditional cockney in the East End of London, which is now more likely to be heard in towns such as Basildon and Harlow, where many East Enders relocated.

Some concerns have, however, emerged over the use of the dialect. At Lilian Baylis school in south London, the patois has been banned from the classroom as part of a government project to improve results. Pupils are taught such dialects are only acceptable in certain circumstances, not including essays or debates. "The language in the formal world of work is standard English," said Gary Phillips, the head teacher. He added, however: "We're not trying to devalue patois, we're trying to teach the kids that there is a time and a place for it."

Steven Swinford and Laura St Quinton in *The Sunday Times*

3 cockney dialect spoken by East Londoners • **3 creole** language with European and African elements • **49 patois** local dialect

b) *Now read again for closer understanding. Use your vocabulary skills to guess what the following phrases mean and draw lines to the same ideas expressed in other words.*

TIP
Does the context help? Do you know another word from the same word family? Is it like German?

1. communicate across the racial divide (ll. 5–6)
2. while it may be baffling (l. 6)
3. through force of numbers with migration (l. 15)
4. on a national basis (ll. 21–22)
5. regardless of their background (ll. 33–34)
6. peppered with different influences (l. 35)
7. concerns have … emerged (l. 47)

a) because so many people immigrate to Britain
b) whatever kind of family they come from
c) talk to people of different ethnic origin
d) affected by many languages
e) people are worried
f) although it is not easy to understand
g) in all parts of the country

2 Find the important information

Go through the text carefully and underline the main points, including any information about the source of the text and who wrote it. Just underline keywords and phrases, not whole sentences.

TIP
The first sentences of paragraphs often express important points.

3 Make notes for the summary →p. 39

[📄] *Make notes, using the points you underlined in the text to guide you. Remember that your summary should be short. Leave out anything which is not really important, and be careful not to include the same idea more than once in your notes, even if it is repeated in the original text.*

TIP
During this step, try to think of your own words to express the content.

4 Write your summary

Use your notes and the phrases from the Word bank to help you. Only look back at the original text if you need to check the content.

WORD BANK
In an article in … • According to the author(s) … • As explained by … • In the opinion of … • to write about/report on … • to say / state / mention (that) … • to make the point that … • to give the example of …

TIP
Depending on the content of your summary, it might be a good idea to divide it into paragraphs.

____

____

____

____

____

____

____

____

____

____

____

____

____

____

____

____

____

____

5 Check your work

[👥] *Use the checklists on page 41 to help you correct your text. Then compare and learn from each other's summaries, e.g. Who managed to present a point in the fewest words? Who found a good way to express an idea in different words? Who used the best structure?*

How to write an argumentative essay →S19

1 Think about the structure

a) *"Does immigration have a positive effect on society?" First put the sentences below in a suitable order to form a short comment. Show the order by writing the numbers 1 to 10 in front of the sentences. (Use a pencil first.) Then examine how the comment is structured. Identify the different parts and write down the sentence numbers on the right.*

Part	Sentences
Introduction: presenting issue	
Main part I: arguments for	
Main part II: arguments against	
Conclusion: final comments	

_____ – To sum up, this is a topic which leads to strong feelings on both sides.

_____ – On the other hand the failure of some immigrants to integrate is criticized.

_____ – One argument often used to support immigration is that it offers advantages to the economy.

_____ – I am sure, however, that the discussion will continue in the future.

_____ – Furthermore, they bring exciting cultural traditions and ideas to their new country.

_____ – In many countries today, immigration has become a big issue in politics.

_____ – Immigrants are usually hard-working and prepared to do jobs other people do not want to do.

_____ – In my opinion, the arguments for immigration are more convincing than those against.

_____ – Different views are expressed about whether or not it has a positive effect on society.

_____ – In addition it is said that immigration causes unemployment and puts pressure on social services.

b) [⎙] *Underline words and phrases which help to structure the content, or which you might be able to use in other comments.*

2 Collect arguments about the issue

*Choose **one** of these questions or statements to write about and note down arguments for and against:*

Older people make better political leaders than young people. • Will people around the world act together in time to stop climate change? • Money cannot buy happiness. • Is it ever right to break the law?

Arguments for: ______________________________

____

Arguments against: ______________________________

____

3 Write your essay →p. 36, p. 41

[▤] *Follow the text structure in ex. 1 and include your arguments from ex. 2, presenting them in a good order. Start a new paragraph for each part of your essay and try to create smooth links. Don't forget to check your text when you have finished.*

WORD BANK

First of all … • First(ly) … / Second(ly) … / … • Finally, … • Last but not least … • The main reason is that … • One / Another (convincing) argument is that … • Furthermore, … • In addition (to) … • It can also be argued that … • To sum up … • In conclusion …

4 Further practice

[⎙] [▤] *Plan and write another argumentative essay on a different topic from the list in ex. 2.*

How to think of ideas for creative writing

1 First decide what kind of ideas you need

Complete the grid with the correct text types. Write down the extra text type on the last line and add your own suggestions for the kind of ideas you should collect.

story • news report • biography • film review • travel writing • diary • formal letter

TIP
Even with non-fictional texts you need to think what kind of ideas could be relevant.

Text type	You might want / need to collect ideas about …
	storyline • cast • technical aspects • positive/negative comments
	person writing • events experienced during the day • reactions/feelings • hopes and fears
	what happened • explanation/background • people involved • reactions and comments
	person writing • person addressed • reason for writing • expectations of answer
	description of place(s) visited • factual information • personal impressions/experiences
	setting • characters • development of plot • turning point • ending

2 Use keywords to help you think

a) *Complete this web of 'character' words that could describe the main character in a story which is set in a school.*

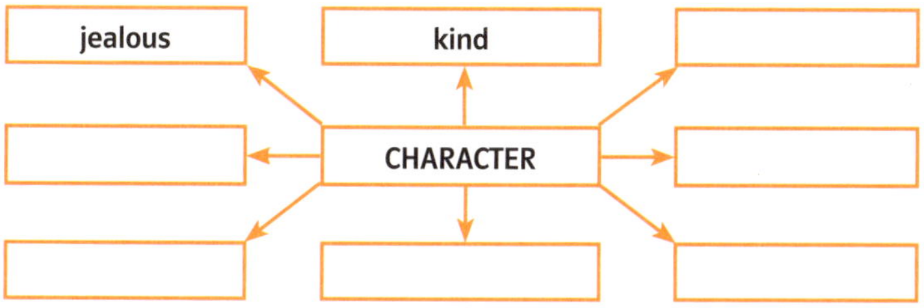

b) *Use some of your words from a) to help you think of possible storylines. Take turns to give a 'character' keyword, and then discuss what the situation could be.*

c) *Now try using the five senses (see, hear, feel, smell, taste) to give you ideas for a text in which someone describes a walk along the coast. Decide for yourself how you want to collect your ideas.*

3 Ask yourself questions

a) *Collect ideas for the content of a letter to a tour operator complaining about a terrible holiday. First work with your partner to make a list of questions you could ask the unhappy customer in order to find out about the holiday and the problem(s). You both write down the same questions in your exercise book, but then work on your own to make up answers to the questions, collecting your ideas in note form. When you have finished it might be interesting to compare the different ideas that have come from the same list of questions.*

b) *Now use the same strategy to collect ideas for a newspaper report to go with the headline: SAVED! This time try working completely on your own.*

TIP
When you think of possible questions you could ask, remember the five Ws: Who? What? When? Where? Why? (Also: How?)

4 Further practice

*Choose **one** of the text types in ex. 1 and develop a web of ideas around a topic of your own choice. (If you like you can then go on to plan and write the text.)*

Linking ideas

Words and phrases that connect your ideas do not only make your text flow smoothly. They also make the content clearer by showing the reader how the ideas relate to one another.

1 Collect useful words and phrases

[📄] *Make a grid like the following. Sort the words and phrases in the box according to how they connect ideas. (You can use your dictionary.) Fill in the grid and add one more word of your own to each group.*

first of all • also • furthermore • similarly • therefore • after • because (of) • in addition (to) • however • so (that) • finally • although • on the other hand • and • previously • as a result • meanwhile • (in order) to • as with • owing to • apart from • (un)like • later • besides

Adding information	Putting ideas or events in order	Expressing cause and effect	Comparing and contrasting

2 Put in suitable connecting words

Use some of the words and phrases from ex. 1 to complete what a British Asian writes. There might be more than one correct answer.

__________ my white friends criticize arranged marriages, most know little about the subject and should __________ not be so quick to judge. __________ answer them, I would like to make a few comments. __________, arranged marriages are not the same as forced marriages. __________ western couples, partners in an arranged marriage make the final decision themselves. __________ the fact that their parents introduced them, __________, they can count on family support. __________, their similar backgrounds give them a good chance of happiness together. __________, I would like to point out that arranged marriages are less likely to end in divorce and, __________, help everyone. __________ the personal unhappiness caused by divorce, family breakdown is __________ expensive for society.

3 Use connectives to create logical links

[📄] *Make sentences, choosing suitable connectives to show how the ideas relate to one another. If necessary, add verbs, articles, pronouns, etc.*

TIP
The subordinate clause can come before or after the main clause.

1. majority of young British Asians live western lifestyle • born in the UK
2. most of older generation accept this • others want to keep to Asian traditions
3. usually no great problems in traditional families • children still young
4. children turn into freedom-loving teenagers • conflict more likely
5. parents try to force their children to obey them • leads to unhappiness
6. sometimes pressure continues to grow • family torn apart

if • while • when • as soon as • although • as • until • because

Using participle constructions → G5

Good written style should be fluent and concise, and using participle constructions can help you to achieve this.

TIP
Remember there are different participle forms.
- **present:** Helping my friend, … (only active meaning)
- **perfect:** Having helped my friend, … / Having been helped by my friend, … (active or passive)
- **past:** Helped by my friend, … (only passive)

1 Put in the correct participles

a) *Complete the information about a famous immigrant.*

Many older black people __________ (live) in the UK can look back on a childhood __________ (spend) in the Caribbean. One such person is Sir Trevor MacDonald, __________ (to be born) in Trinidad in 1939. __________ (come) from a poor family, he had little formal education but always loved English, __________ (read) widely and __________ (listen) to the BBC World Service. __________ (begin) his career as a journalist with the local media in Trinidad, he then joined the BBC's Caribbean team before __________ (relocate) to the UK in 1969 to work for BBC Radio. In 1973 he accepted a job __________ (offer) by Independent Television News. There, __________ (work) his way up, he became the first black news presenter on British television. __________ (consider) to speak perfect English, he won great respect. Every evening millions of people watched him __________ (present) the news. __________ (contribute) so much to British journalism over the years, he was given the title 'Sir' in 1999.

b) *Talk about the participle constructions in the text. Say how you would have to express the same ideas in English without participles. Also think how you would translate the participle constructions into German.*

2 Rewrite the sentences with participle constructions

Turn the marked words into participle constructions.

1. Many new immigrants **who arrive** in the east of England are from eastern Europe.
2. Some need to find work right away **because they have brought** little or no money with them.
3. They are often prepared to do jobs **that are not wanted** by other people.
4. **When they hear** about places where there is the chance of farm work, they go there very early in the morning.
5. They stand in the meeting points until a van or minibus comes to bring them to a farm. **They are waiting**.
6. They work all day in the fields. **They pick** vegetables.

3 Give the information more fluently and concisely

Mark where you can link or shorten sentences with participles. Then rewrite the text.

In the past, everyone who held a British passport had the right to live in the UK, and after World War II, because of the extra workers that were needed in the British economy, there was mass immigration. Blacks and Asians entered the country in great numbers. They mainly settled in the big cities. Because many white people were worried by the idea of a large black community, they started to protest. They said they did not want to watch while their British way of life disappeared. Racial prejudice was common, and when immigrants were looking for homes or jobs, they often experienced verbal and even physical abuse. The government was put under pressure and had to act. After it had introduced stricter immigration rules, it tried to improve race relations through laws that protected ethnic minorities. Discrimination continued for a long time, however. It made life hard for non-white citizens.

Writing in the appropriate style

The style of language should match the type of text you are writing, so think about the vocabulary and sentence structures you use. Remember to keep to the same style throughout the text.

TIP
A good dictionary will tell you if a word or phrase is especially formal or informal.

1 Formal and informal vocabulary

a) *Find six pairs with the same meaning and write them in the correct list in the grid.*

in my view • wicked • meeting • furthermore • wonderful • OK • if you ask me • satisfactory • encounter • know a lot • and another thing • be well-informed

More formal	Less formal

b) *Talk about the words on the right. Is the style more formal or informal? What alternative word could you use to change the register?*

kids • attend • a host of • authorize • scary

2 Change spoken style to written style

Read what different people say and rewrite the sentences in the appropriate style for a factual text. Replace the informal expressions with suitable words and phrases, also making any other changes you think necessary.

TIP
Formal style usually expresses ideas more exactly than informal style.

1. "My grandma came here way back in the 70s."
____
2. "She found it, like, so hard at first, 'cos it – well, England was the total opposite of St Lucia."
____
3. "She got a job OK, but she had to listen to, you know, racial abuse from her boss."
____
4. "But she's not one to give up, and she did loads of courses and stuff so she could be a nurse."
____
5. "She did pretty well in her career, actually, and went on even after she had my mother."
____

3 Correct the register

Read the article and mark anything that is not the appropriate style for a written factual text. Then rewrite the whole text, making the necessary improvements.

Racist police?

Statistics show that cops stop and search young black guys in the street more often than any other group in the population. Some people say it stinks and complain that the police are racist. The police say no. They point to other statistics showing that this group is more likely to be responsible for bad stuff involving knives and guns. In their view, their actions help to protect the public – and that means the black community, too – against street violence. But anyway, they do agree that their relations with some citizens are not always too great. They are therefore doing things to recruit more police officers from ethnic minorities. At the moment it's like only white people are in a position of power.

Expressing information in your own words

Except for quotations, you should never copy anyone else's words. It is therefore important to be able to express information in your own words when you write a summary or take facts from a text you use for research.

1 Use words with a similar meaning

Using a dictionary if necessary, write down an alternative for each of the marked words. Make sure that the word is correct in the context.

TIP
An English-English dictionary is best when you want to find a synonym.

1. The majority of Asians are **prepared** to work hard. – ____________________
2. The **concept** of 'family' is also important to them. – ____________________
3. These attitudes help to explain their **achievements** in the UK. – ____________________
4. Many families **found** their own business. – ____________________

5. Relatives all work together to help the business **grow**. – ____________________
6. This brings **benefits** for themselves and for the country. – ____________________
7. Some of the **most prosperous** British citizens are Asian. – ____________________
8. Their businesses also **add** to the UK economy. – ____________________

2 Find a simpler expression

Draw lines to match the phrases on the left with the same meaning expressed in simpler words.

1. diverse forms of employment	• personal hopes
2. less than welcoming environment	• all kinds of work
3. individual aspirations	• bad luck
4. a series of unfortunate events	• many reasons
5. enormous financial consequences	• unfriendly place
6. a host of contributory factors	• high cost

TIP
Although there may be lots of long or difficult words in the texts you read, simple English can also be good formal written style!

3 Write new sentences

a) *Think of a different way to express the information below, keeping to a suitable style of language for a factual text.*

1. There has been a Chinese community in Britain since the early 19th century.
2. They have settled in widespread geographical locations.
3. The majority are well-integrated into British society.
4. They also enjoy an active ethnic life.
5. Educational achievement among young Chinese is generally high.
6. The Chinese have one of the highest inter-ethnic marriage rates.

b) *Compare your new versions for each of the sentences in a). Check that you have both given the correct facts in your own words and that the style is appropriate.*

Using interesting vocabulary

Always try to use words that give the exact meaning or create a clear image or atmosphere for the reader. This is especially important in creative writing.

1 Think of adjectives with a specific meaning

Words with a general meaning like 'nice', 'bad' or 'big' are not very interesting. Think how you could describe the following nouns more exactly. Write down two possible adjectives for each noun, trying not to use any adjective more than once.

1. a nice …	2. a bad …	3. a big …
meal: ____________	accident: ____________	hole: ____________
film: ____________	smell: ____________	noise: ____________
hairstyle: ____________	mood: ____________	journey: ____________
person: ____________	result: ____________	decision: ____________

2 Add adjectives and adverbs to improve the text

First read the whole text. Then go back and add your own ideas to create stronger images.

Wasim walked ____________ onto the pitch, holding up his ____________ bat to greet the ____________ crowd. Playing cricket for England was no longer just a ____________ dream! He could feel his heart jumping ____________ while he waited for his first ball. It came at him ____________ like a shot from a gun, but he took a ____________ step towards it and hit it ____________. Everyone cheered as the ball flew ____________ from his bat into the crowd. "Wasim! Wasim!" He could hear them shouting ____________. – "Wasim!" Wasim's ____________ teacher finally brought his ____________ daydream to an end. "You won't learn to speak French ____________ by staring out of the window at that ____________ cricket pitch!"

3 Collect verbs that express extra information

a) *Think of verbs you could use instead of 'say' and 'go' to give more than just the basic meaning.*

1. say: ____
2. go: ____

b) [⏎] [▤] *Make up your own sentences using four verbs from each of your lists in a).*

4 Bring ideas to life with metaphors

[▤] *Write at least eight imaginative sentences about nature.*

Example: The wind cried and complained through the cracks in the walls.

TIP
The sounds of words can help to create atmosphere, too, especially in poems.

wind • mountain • sun • waves • flowers • clouds • earth • …

\+

lick • smile • wake • nod • guard • dance • sleep • dance • hide • grab • hurry • …

Checking and improving texts (I)

Always check and double-check the texts you write. Try to develop an awareness of the type of mistakes you make most often so that you can pay special attention to them. Ask a partner to help you, too.
It is often easier to see mistakes and weaknesses in an unfamiliar text.

Checklist A	Checklist B
Look for mistakes in:	**Make sure your text has:**
• spelling	• a clear, logical content
• irregular verb forms	• the appropriate style
• word order	• a good choice of vocabulary
• grammar	• smooth links
• punctuation	• no unnecessary repetition

TIP
Apart from looking at the language critically, look at the text as a whole. Check that it keeps to the rules for that type of text e.g. a summary should be short; an argumentative essay should present arguments for both sides; a factual text should state facts, not your opinions, etc.

1 Correct the mistakes in the text

Use Checklist A above to help you. Mark anything that is wrong and write the corrections above the text.

When students at Shireland Academy in birmingham telled their teacher Mandeep Atwal they want to talk more about the race and religion, she decided starting a project called 'Young Voices'. Now has the school a discussion group wear everyone can speak free about sensitive issues related on these topics. Miss Atwal has also created a website on the schools computer network. This website give students, which come from many ethnic minoritys, the opportunity to present their own back ground and experiences. For example, a Christian girl has given informations about his church, some Muslim boys have posted a video over knife crime, and a group of Afro-Caribbean students have wrote about the stereotyping of black people in media. Everyone agrees that the 'Young Voices' project has been a big success students have found out about himself and others at their school, and some have even learned to perform music and danceing from each other's cultures. This has helped them to mix good and make friends with people they did not speak usually to in the past.

2 Improve the following paragraph

Use Checklist B above to help you. Mark the text to show the improvements you want to make. Then write your new version. When you have finished, explain the changes you have made to your partner.

TIP
For this text, you needn't worry about the points in Checklist A.

New figures given by the government give new information. They show that almost 22 percent of students at British primary schools and 18 percent in secondary schools belong to ethnic minorities. One in eight students do not speak English as a first language. But it isn't the same in all parts of the country. The proportion of kids from minority groups is especially high in London. There there are six black or Asian students for every four from white families. Non-white students form a majority in schools in Birmingham, Leicester, Luton and Slough. In some areas school populations are almost completely white. In Devon 95 percent of students are white British. Yesterday the government minister for schools spoke about the statistics. He gave his opinion about them. He said it was important to teach good race relations in all kinds of schools throughout the country. And he said children whose English wasn't too good would get extra help.

Speaking skills

How to prepare and give a short campaign speech →S28

1 Explain the structure of a campaign speech

Add the correct functions to the different parts of a speech.

present facts about the problem • summarize your main points • win the audience's attention • ask everyone to support the campaign • state what you are campaigning about • explain what you think needs to be done

Introduction: ______________________

Main part: ______________________

Conclusion: ______________________

2 Discuss different ways to begin a speech

[👥] *With a partner talk about these possible beginnings for a speech about vegetarianism. Say how you think the audience is likely to react to the speaker, and why. (There is no one correct answer – just your opinion!)*

1. "Ladies and gentlemen, I'd like to talk to you about becoming a vegetarian."
2. "Hi, I'm Mike and I have a question. If you love animals called pets, why do you eat animals called dinner?"
3. "Good evening, everyone. Did you know that eating one pound of hamburger does the same environmental damage as driving a car for three weeks?"
4. "Hello. What a friendly-looking audience! But sorry, as a vegetarian I can't say it's nice to 'meat' you! Ha ha!"

3 Find out about the issue of an unequal world

The following statements are taken from a campaign booklet by 'Friends of the Earth'. Mark the information about problems in red, and the ideas for possible solutions in blue.

- Globally the richer countries are using up more than their fair share of natural resources like energy, water, timber and minerals.
- Strong laws could make companies responsible for their impact on communities and the environment worldwide.
- Over 1 billion people survive on less than US $1 a day.
- Global trade rules and the power of big businesses over governments are doing little to make life better for the world's majority.
- Buying fairly traded products such as coffee, tea, chocolate and bananas puts money back into local communities.
- Friends of the Earth is campaigning for global rules that protect the planet and give local communities priority over so-called free trade.
- Just 500 big companies now control two-thirds of world trade.
- Global bodies like the World Bank finance projects like oil pipelines and mines that are a danger to local water supplies, land and homes.
- Each of us can reduce our negative impact on the planet and other people by thinking about how we use resources.
- The richest 20 % of the world's population consume 86 % of its resources.

4 Plan your speech

Look back at ex. 1, and then write notes for a short speech campaigning for a fairer world. The information and ideas from ex. 3 can help you with the content for the main part, but think of your own ideas for the introduction and conclusion.

TIP
Develop the main part of the speech logically. Find a good order for the points you make.

Introduction: ______________________________

____

Main part: ______________________________

____

____

____

____

____

____

Conclusion: ______________________________

____

5 Think how to deliver a speech

a) [👥] *Work with a partner to collect a few tips about body language and how to use your voice.*

____

____

____

____

b) [🗨] *In class, talk about how you can stress important points you want to make in a speech. Think of different strategies that can help: tone of voice, length of sentences, giving the audience time to think, etc.*

6 Practise and give your speech →p. 47

a) *Think how you can use some of the phrases in the Word bank to help you communicate your ideas from ex. 4 to an audience. Then practise giving your speech. Try to speak fluently and remember the tips about voice and body language. Keep practising until you only need a quick look at your notes from time to time.*

b) [👥👥] *Take turns to give your speeches. Listen carefully to each other and give constructive criticism. Check ex. 4 on page 13 to see if you have managed to improve your weak points.*

WORD BANK

Presenting an issue:
Let me give you some facts. • First of all, … • Did you know that …? • The problem/truth is that …

Suggesting ideas:
What we need is/are … • One/Another solution would be … • It's very important to … • We should …

Calling for action:
Please … • I'm asking you to … • You can make a difference by … • Help to campaign for …

How to present film material →S11

TIP
The first time you watch film material, just try to get the gist. Don't write anything down until you have finished watching.

1 Find out basic information

[🎬] Watch the video once. Then in one or two sentences explain what kind of film it is and what it is about.

____

____

2 Identify the audio-visual elements

[🎬] [♪] Check the following words and phrases, and underline all the elements used in the video. You can watch the video as often as necessary.

voice-over • photo • interview • film clip • studio presenter • cartoon • background music • map • caption • diagram

3 Analyze the video

a) *[🎬] First focus on the spoken information. Find the correct order for the notes on the right and enter them in the first column of the grid below.*

b) *[🎬] In the second column write down what you can see on screen while listening to the information. (Ex. 2 can help you.)*

- pros and cons of nuclear power
- energy problems in the UK
- tips for using less energy
- how nuclear power works
- list of different energy sources

Order	Spoken information:	What you see on screen:
1		
2		
3		
4		
5		

c) *[👥] Use the grid and the phrases from the Word bank to talk about the connection between the spoken information and what you see on screen.*

WORD BANK
to introduce • to lead into • helpful to know who/what … • to show/illustrate • easier to remember/understand • to stress what is said • summary of the main points • to make clear/interesting • to get/keep the viewer's attention

4 Prepare and give your presentation

a) *Follow these instructions to help you write notes for a short presentation of the video.*

What kind of film is it? → What is it about? → Who gives the spoken information? → What is the function of the visual elements? → What is your opinion of the video, and why?

____

____

____

b) *[👥👤] Work in groups to present the video. Tell each other what you think is good or not so good about your presentations.*

How to take part in an informal discussion → S26

1 Make yourself familiar with the issue

a) *"Each household in the country should only be allowed to own one car." Think carefully about what the speaker is saying. In note form, collect arguments that could be made for and against the statement. These ideas might help:*

effect on environment • public transport • size of household • type of car • right to personal freedom • …

Arguments for: ______	Arguments against: ______
______	______
______	______
______	______

b) *Now use the arguments you collected to help you form an opinion. In one short sentence, sum up your reaction to the statement made by the speaker in a).*

______

______

TIP
In a discussion, it helps to be prepared for arguments the other side might make.

2 Check how a discussion develops

a) [👥] *With a partner, talk about how the marked phrases help to link the following speakers and help their discussion to develop. (Reading out the discussion without these phrases will also help you to understand their importance.)*

- "**I think** the government should do more to stop people flying."
- "**I totally agree.** Air travel does a lot of damage to the environment."
- "**Well, that may be true, but** other forms of transport are equally bad."
- "**Sorry, I have to correct you there.** The fact is, it's much greener to travel by train."
- "**Another point is that** trains are relatively quiet. Planes create noise pollution, too."
- "**Too right.** They make a terrible noise. I'd hate to live right next to an airport."
- "**OK, but the problem is,** if there were no planes, it would take ages to get to faraway places."

b) [👥] *Go through the discussion in a) again and replace the marked words with an alternative phrase from the Word bank below.*

3 Hold your discussion → p. 48, p. 49

[👥👥] *Work in groups of three or four in which not everyone agrees on the statement in ex. 1. One of you starts the discussion by expressing a reaction to the statement, and then the others join in. Try to make your points convincingly and to express yourselves appropriately.*

4 Further practice

[👥👥] [📝] *Work in groups to discuss this statement:*

"It's unrealistic to expect people to change to cycling as their regular form of transport."

WORD BANK

Expressing an opinion:
I think / believe … • In my opinion, … • As I see it, … • It seems clear to me that …

Agreeing:
Exactly / Absolutely. • I agree (with you). • You're (so) right. • I share your view completely.

Disagreeing:
I disagree / don't agree. • Sorry, but (I think) that's wrong. • I see it differently. • That's not right / correct.

Partly accepting:
Possibly, but … • Even if that's so, … • Yes, but on the other hand … • Although you've got a point, …

Introducing a new point:
It's also important to remember that … • I'd like to raise the point that … • A further argument for / against … • One thing that hasn't been mentioned yet is …

How to develop a good conversation →S25

1 Match the topic to the situation and conversation partner

Use the suggested colour and underline the topics you think are suitable for each situation. (You may want to underline the same topic more than once, and there may be topics you don't underline at all.)

1. chat with a friend (blue)
2. conversation with a stranger (red)
3. job interview (green)

weather • health • interests • place you are in • families • political views • ambitions • entertainment • news • the environment • travel • gossip

2 Build on what the other person says

a) [⏍] *Put the sentences in the right order to make a conversation between two strangers in a café.*

1. ____ 2. ____ 3. ____ 4. ____ 5. ____ 6. ____ 7. ____ 8. ____

A: That's what I thought when I saw the menu outside. I'm new here.
B: It's very busy, isn't it? Do you come here often?
C: Yes, I moved here from London last week.
D: Excuse me. May I sit at this table with you?
E: Quite often, yes. There's always a good choice of tasty dishes.
F: Only last week, eh? Well, I think you'll find it a good place to live.
G: New in this town, you mean?
H: Yes, of course. It's always hard to find a seat in this café.

b) [ꙋꙋ] [⏍] *Act out the conversation in a). Learn your role by heart, so you can concentrate on listening, reacting, and using friendly body language.*

TIP
Learn to recognize signals that tell you it is your turn to speak: a question, a pause, a suggestion, or a statement that invites a question from you.

3 Show interest

Think of comments you could make to show these conversation partners you are interested in what they are saying.

1. "There's a documentary about alternative energy sources on TV this evening."

   You: ____________________

2. "I see the forecast is for sun again tomorrow – but it'll probably rain on Saturday and Sunday."

   You: ____________________

3. "It's terrible that so many people in developing countries have no access to health services."

   You: ____________________

4 Practise conversations →p. 47, p. 48

[ꙋꙋ] *Choose from the situations below and develop two short conversations (1–2 minutes each).*
Prepare by making a few notes about the person you are playing and what you might want to say.
Use the appropriate register and try to speak fluently.
The phrases from the Word bank can help you to start and finish the conversation.

WORD BANK
Starting a conversation:
Hi / Hello. • Good morning / afternoon / evening. • Excuse me. • Just the person I wanted to see! • I'm / My name is … • How are you? • Can I / you …? • So tell me …
Bringing a conversation to an end:
Well, it's been nice talking to you. • I'm afraid I must go now. • Hey, look at the time! • Thanks for the help / information. • See you soon / later. • All the best. • Bye / Goodbye.

1. An office worker talks to a new colleague.
2. Two friends arriving at school on Monday morning chat about the weekend.
3. A local person helps a tourist by giving information.
4. A teenager sees an adult neighbour in the street.

Speaking fluently and naturally

Whatever register you use in conversations, dialogues or speeches, you should try to make your English as smooth and natural as possible. The exercises on this page show you some ways to do this.

1 Link ideas

[📄] Make these speakers at a village meeting sound more fluent by linking the pairs of sentences to make one longer sentence. You can do this in any way you like (conjunction, infinitive, participle, …) as long as the correct meaning is expressed. When you have finished, compare your ideas with a partner.

1. "We need to organize a campaign. We must stop the plans for that new motorway."
2. "It won't be easy to win the fight. I'm sure we can do it."
3. "Nobody here wants to listen to all that traffic. It'll roar past all night."
4. "I can help to get the media involved on our side. I work in that field."

2 Use 'fillers'

a) *Read the dialogue and mark the words or phrases which would not be used in written English, but which help to make this informal spoken style more natural.*

TIP
Fillers give you time to think about what you want to say.

A: So, what do you think about the plans for a community garden?
B: Well, I think it's, yeah, it's a great idea.
A: Good. But it's quite a big project, you see, and we do need volunteers.
B: Sure, and I mean, I'd like to help. The thing is, I'm, er, really busy with work at the moment. Also, I have absolutely no idea how to, you know, plant trees or whatever.
A: Oh, that isn't a problem. Anyway, can I at least put your name down as a possible helper?
B: Hm, I'm not sure. I, um, I think it might be better to ask somebody else. Sorry.

b) *[👥] Act out the dialogue in a). Try to speak fluently, but also think where you need to make natural pauses.*

c) *[✍] [📄] Rewrite this dialogue, adding a few fillers to make it sound more natural.*

A: Why are we going to get a third bin for our rubbish? It's crazy!
B: It's so we can collect different things for recycling.
A: I only have a tiny garden. I don't have the space for three bins.
B: Maybe you should phone the council and ask for advice.
A: That might be an idea. If they try to deliver an extra bin, I won't take it.

3 Add phrases that help to organize and explain

Complete the beginning of a speech with suitable words and phrases from the box. (Not all the phrases are needed.)

basically • and so on • in other words • obviously • last but not least • first of all • on the other hand • the point is

"____________________, I'd like to explain what our charity is about. ____________________, we try to educate young people about the environment. ____________________, today's children are tomorrow's adults – ____________________, the people who will be making decisions in the future. So ____________________ they need to learn about issues like energy sources, rainforests, healthy food, ____________________. We do our work in a number of ways, offering free school talks, online information and ____________________ fun environmental courses."

Expressing oneself appropriately

You always need to be aware of the appropriate language register, depending on the situation and who you are talking to. In English it is also important to express yourself politely in order not to risk offending people.

TIP
A friendly face and tone of voice also help good communication!

1 Use the right register

a) *Complete the grid by filling in the missing expression. (There is more than one possible solution.)*

b) [📄] *Change the register of this short exchange from informal to formal.*

A: Hey, you!
B: Who? Me?
A: Yeah. Don't you want your bag of apples? Here – you left them on the stall.
B: Silly me. Thanks, mate.
A: No problem.

Formal expression	Informal expression
Good morning.	
	Wow, cool!
	Thanks, mate.
I do apologize.	
You're welcome.	
	See you. / Bye.

2 Be polite

These speakers in a discussion sound very rude. Use the phrases in the Word bank to help you rewrite what they say more politely.

WORD BANK
I'm afraid … • With respect, … • Would you mind …? • Sorry, but … • Please allow me to … • If I may, … • Excuse me, but …

1. "You must be crazy if that's what you think. You're so wrong!"

____

2. "I'm fed up with you interrupting me! Wait till I've finished what I'm trying to say."

____

3. "You've been talking for ages. Why don't you shut up and give somebody else the chance to speak?"

____

4. "You aren't making any sense at all. You're just talking rubbish that has nothing to do with the issue."

____

3 Avoid offending people

Write down what you could say to make the following people change how they behave. Think about the situation, who you are talking to and therefore how tactful you need to be.

TIP
People are more likely to do what you want if you express yourself tactfully.

1. to a neighbour who always uses throwaway plastic bags: _______________

____

2. to a stranger who doesn't clean up the mess his dog makes in the street: _______________

____

3. to a member of the family who forgot to turn off the light – again: _______________

____

Making a point

When you make a point in a discussion, it is important to express yourself clearly and convincingly.

1 Speak in a way that is easy to follow

TIP
Start with the main idea. Avoid repetition, vague language and very long sentences.

a) [👥] *Read the tip and then comment on how these speakers make their points during a discussion about their local environment.*

1. "One thing makes me really angry. I'm talking about litter – I mean dropping it in the street. People shouldn't drop litter, should they? So there, that's the point I'd like to make."
2. "My opinion is that I think we need more trees so the city would look greener and also the air quality would be better, too, and it would be a big improvement. So anyway, we should plant more trees and make the city greener."

b) [📄] *Rewrite the points made by the speakers in a), making them shorter and easier to follow.*

2 Support opinions with facts

a) [📄] *Make a grid like the one on the right and sort these phrases into two groups.*

Stating an opinion	Supporting an opinion

A good example is … • It has been proved that … • I believe … • The fact is, … • In my opinion / view, … • To my mind, … • Statistics / Surveys show … • Personally, I think … • In my own experience, … • It seems to me that …

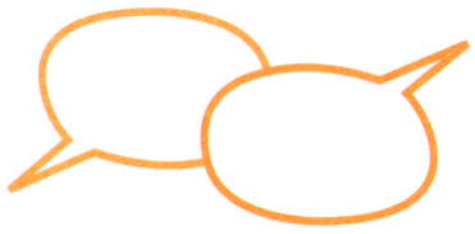

b) *Choose suitable phrases from a) to complete what these people say.*

"________________ people need to wake up to the dangers of global warming. ________________ sea levels are rising all around the world." – "Yes, ________________ people just don't understand the need to reduce their CO_2 emissions. ________________ the way they go on driving around in cars instead of using greener forms of transport." – "________________ the government should do more to educate the population. ________________ not everyone even accepts that climate change is happening."

3 Add stress

a) [✍] *Underline the words and phrases which help to give stress to what this speaker says.*

"It does seem crazy to waste natural resources on materials that just get thrown away. It's packaging that I'm thinking of. I sometimes buy things with unnecessary packaging myself, but it's really very difficult not to. No way should we let this situation continue. As consumers, we ourselves can help by putting pressure on shops not to sell products with extra packaging. What we also need is a complete ban on plastic bags."

b) [✍] [📄] *Rewrite this point, adding stress with some of the ways you identified in a).*

"I believe a lot of people are simply too lazy to help the environment. I can't accept their argument that as individuals they don't have any influence. The fact is, all of us working together can make a big difference. We need action on a global scale."

Expressing statistical information

Statistics are often written down in abbreviated form, so if you want to give this information in spoken English, it is important to know what the abbreviations stand for and how to say them.

1 Numbers

[⏍] *Identify the mistakes in the way the numbers are spoken, and rewrite them correctly.*

1. "In an average week I drive three hundred fifty miles." – ____________
2. "The biggest city on earth is Tokyo, with over twenty-eight millions people." – ____________
3. "For information about recycling, phone four six nil double eight two." – ____________
4. "The protest meeting about the wind farm lasted for four and half hours." – ____________
5. "Friends of the Earth was started in one thousand nine hundred and seventy-one." – ____________
6. "I read that Germany has one comma three per cent of the world's population." – ____________

2 Measurements

Find an abbreviation in the box for each type of measurement, and write down how you say it in words.

6 ft 2 in • 3½ l • 5 sq. km • 12 hrs • 40 mph • 150 g • 31° C • 5.5 %

1. time: ____________
2. area: ____________
3. temperature: ____________
4. speed: ____________
5. height: ____________
6. proportion: ____________
7. volume: ____________
8. weight: ____________

3 Talking about facts and figures

Use the words on the right to complete this text from a leaflet campaigning for vegetarianism.

factors • higher • per • twice as much • rise • on average • this figure • approximately • less • add • growing number • percent • compared to • as a result • statistics

In 2008 there were ____________ 6.5 billion people living on Earth. By 2050 ____________ is expected to ____________ to 9 million, and ____________ more food will be needed. Farming already uses up 20 to 30 ____________ of the world's resources of land, water and energy, and such ____________ mean that future food production will ____________ to the pressure on the environment. Meat causes the most damage. ____________ vegetarian foods, meat has a much ____________ environmental cost. In spite of this, ____________ show that ____________, we eat ____________ meat today as 50 years ago (43 kgs ____________ person). This is madness. If we were all vegetarians, there would be ____________ environmental damage – and we might have a better chance of feeding the ____________ of hungry people in the world.

Interpreting diagrams → S35

Different kinds of diagrams can be used to present statistics clearly in very little space.
When you interpret these diagrams, you need to be able to put this visual information into words.

1 Useful phrases

Find the correct headings for the groups of phrases below. (Two headings are not needed.)

Making comparisons • Making predictions • Expressing quantity • Describing trends • Expressing cause and effect

WORD BANK

____

- a large / small amount of …
- … percent of …
- the (large) majority of …
- the figure / percentage for … is …

____

- more / less / fewer than …
- the most / least
- twice / three times as much as …
- compared to …

____

- to rise / fall / go up / go down
- has / have been growing since / for …
- a sharp / dramatic / … rise / fall
- the rate of growth / change / …

2 A pie chart

a) *Write one sentence explaining what the pie chart is about.*

b) *Choose from the phrases in ex. 1 to help you write three sentences based on the information in the pie chart.*

c) *Comment on the information. Does anything surprise you? Do you think the water usage shown in the chart is similar to the one in your own home?*

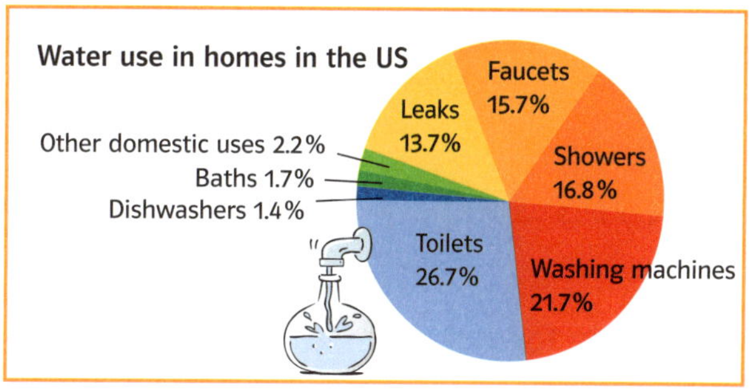

3 A line graph and a bar graph

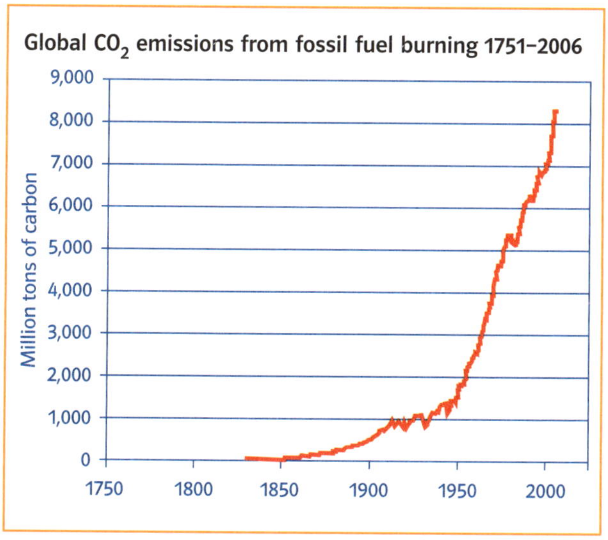

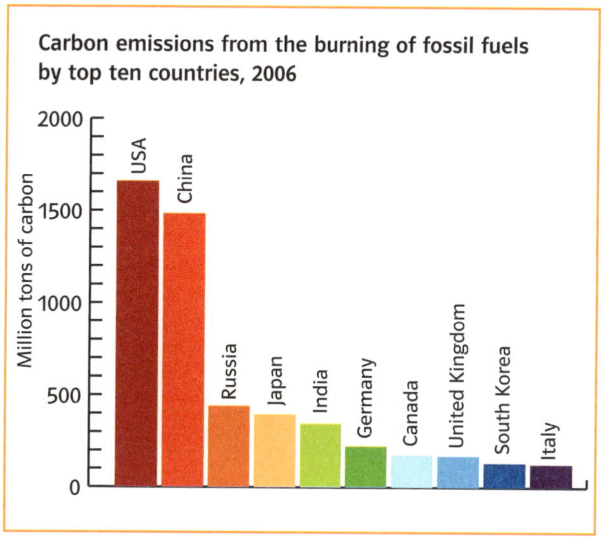

a) *Sum up the main information in the line graph in one or two sentences.*

b) *With a partner talk about how the bar graph is related to the line graph. Also collect ideas about why there is such a big difference between the countries. Say what factors you think could be involved.*

c) *Draw your own diagram to present this information: Producing electricity creates 40 % of global carbon emissions from fossil fuel burning, while transportation is responsible for 21 % and industry for 17 %. Household and commercial activities account for a further 14 % of emissions, and the rest comes from a variety of other sources.*

Listening skills

Listening for gist and for detail: A news report →S29

1 Preparing to listen

a) *You are going to watch a video and listen to information about children like the boy in the picture. Make notes about your expectations. Where does he live? What is his situation?*

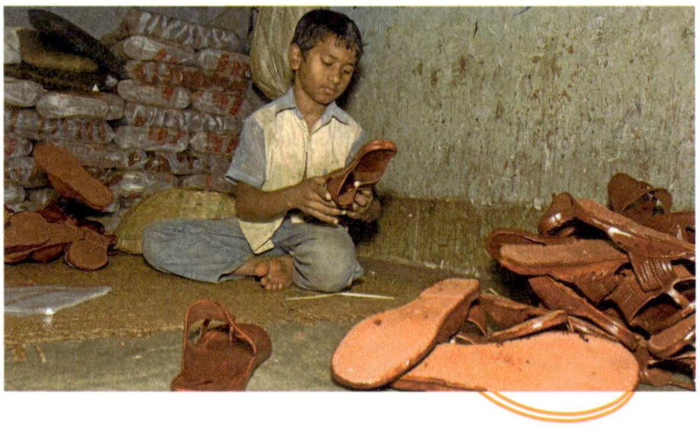

____

____

____

b) [🎬] *Now watch the news report without the sound. Correct your notes from a) if necessary. Write down what you think the gist of the recording might be. Remember it should be one sentence or phrase which sums up the main contents. (At this stage you can make several guesses. Write them one under the other in a list.)*

____

____

____

2 Listening for gist

[🎬] *Watch the whole recording. Concentrate on information about the people and the places. Are there keywords which are repeated? Make notes on these points first, if you like, then write down the gist of the recording in one sentence. If you do not feel able to do this yet, listen to the whole recording again as often as you like.*

TIP
Remember the question words that can help you to find out the main ideas: Who? • What? • When? • Where? • Why • How?

____

____

3 Listening for detail

a) [🎬] *Watch the news report in sections and find the answers to these questions. (They are in chronological order.)*

TIP
If you want to improve your listening skills, you must be patient! Be prepared to listen to a tricky part of the text several times. If you're still having problems, go on to the next section and come back to the problem later.

1. How many child workers are there in Dhaka?

____

2. How old is Ibrahim? ______________________________________
3. How much money does Saddam earn? ______________________________________
4. How long does he work? ______________________________________
5. What are the boys in the second room doing? ______________________________________

____

6. Who is the man in the office? ______

7. What does he say about the 8-year-old working in the factory? ______

______

8. What does UNICEF organize in Dhaka? ______

______

9. What is their strategy called? ______

b) [video] *Watch the video again and find the information you need to answer these questions. (You may have to listen more than once and make notes first.)*

1. What is the legal position on child labour in Bangladesh? ______

______

2. Why does Ibrahim think he is "lucky"? ______

______

3. Why doesn't Saddam go to school? ______

______

4. Why is the work of the boys in the second room particularly dangerous? ______

______

5. Why does the reporter mention Charles Dickens? ______

______

6. What is different in the workplace organized by UNICEF? ______

______

4 Listening for gist and for detail

a) [CD] *Listen to the extract of a BBC radio programme which was broadcast in October 2006. How many speakers do you hear? Which varieties of English do you recognize?*

b) [CD] *Listen again and find out who or what is at the centre of the news. Make notes, then write down the gist of the recording in one sentence.*

______

______

______

______

TIP
Here are two names which you will hear:
Muhammad Yunus • Grameen Bank

c) [◎] [⊡] *Listen again and complete this summary.*

Professor Yunus told Roland Burke the prize meant a great deal to him and to ______________________ ______________. A large crowd gathered at ______________________________. Members of the bank's staff ______________________________. Micro-credit means offering ______________________________ to the poor so that they ______________________________. ______________________________ ago, Mr Yunus gave his first loan of less than ______________________________ to a group of ______________________________. Grameen Bank now has more than ______________________________. Yunus' message is that nobody in this world should ______________________________.

d) [◎] [⊡] *Listen again. Make notes about*

- *who Mr Yunus is,*
- *why he has been awarded the prize,*
- *his reactions to the news,*
- *his future plans and visions.*

Listen to the text again as often as necessary and add to your notes.

TIP
Try to listen to news reports in English as often as possible. (The online versions of newspapers often have audios and videos.) Start with news topics which are familiar to you from the German media.

____

____

____

____

____

e) [👥] *Use your notes to give your own oral summary to a partner.*

Listening for gist and for detail: A radio interview → S29

1 Preparing to listen

Before you listen, think what is special about an interview. In what way is it different from other conversations between two people?

____

____

2 Listening for gist

a) [◎] *You are going to listen to two extracts from an interview with Evan Williams, one of the co-founders of the Internet service Twitter. Listen to both parts and fill in the information about the two speakers.*

	Name	Accent
Interviewer		
Interviewee		

b) [◎] [◫] *Listen to the interview. Which two subjects does Evan talk about? Tick the right answers.*

- the danger of government interference with the Internet ☐
- the problems facing Internet services in authoritarian countries ☐
- the positive effect of Internet services like Twitter ☐
- the problems of finding investors in new technologies ☐

c) [◎] *Now listen to the interview again and write down the gist of what Evan says about his firm.*

3 Listening for detail

a) [◎] *Listen to the interview again. Find these quotes and, in your own words, explain what Evan means.*

1. "The open exchange of information has a positive impact on the world."

What examples does Evan give for this positive impact?

2. "So Twitter is causing some waves in those regions."

What details do Evan and the interviewer give about these "waves"?

TIP
When you've finished all the tasks, it's a good idea to go back to your summary of the gist. Now you can see how much better you understand the text after all your patient work on it!

b) [◎] [◫] *Listen to the interview again. What does Evan say about the financial aspects of his business (buying and selling, making money, …)?*

Listening for gist and for detail: Real conversations →S29

1 Preparing to listen

a) *In one sentence say what this cartoon is about.*

TIP
Analyzing visual material can often help you to understand texts, written or spoken. Cartoonists in particular often try to make you think about a topic, maybe in a way you hadn't thought of before.

b) *What feelings do people usually want to show with their bumper stickers?*

c) [👥] *Now deal with the cartoon in detail. Make notes, then discuss the message of the cartoon with a partner.*

2 Listening to a discussion on the same topic

a) [◎] *Listen to the dialogue between two high-school students, Carrie and Jordan. Make brief notes on the gist.*

b) [◎] [✎] [▤] *Make a grid like the following. Then listen again and make notes on Jordan's questions and Carrie's answers.*

Jordan's questions	Carrie's answers

c) [◎] [✎] *Listen again. Make notes on Carrie's arguments, then use them to tell your partner what she thinks. (Do you need to make notes about what Jordan says?)*

d) [👥] [✎] *What would Carrie say about the Apathy Club? Discuss your ideas with a partner.*

Taking notes while listening →S30

1 Take short notes →p. 16

Read these notes on the extract from Prime Minister Rudd's speech which you listened to in Part A. Rewrite them in a shorter form, using any symbols or abbreviations which you find useful. (You can listen to the extract again, if you like.)

TIP
It is important to keep your notes short so that you have enough time to go on listening. Here are some examples:

- Mr Rudd wanted to apologize … → R: "Sorry"
- They had no parents, brothers, … → without family
- for example → e.g.
- very good → …

1. Mr Rudd • offers apology to children who were taken from families and put into institutions

____

2. these children • often endured physical suffering and emotional starvation

____

3. after leaving homes / institutions children had no chance of success in outside world • no family or friends to help them

____

4. many other children • brought from other countries, told they were orphans and other lies; separated from brothers and sisters

____

2 Write notes in the correct order

a) [◎] [ጸጸ] *Listen to another extract from the same speech made by the Australian Prime Minister. Make notes about the gist. Compare your results with a partner.*

____

____

____

b) [◎] *Here are some notes taken about the speech. Listen again and number the notes in the correct order.*

- recognize pain suffered ☐
- protect children = duty – all ☐
- thanks to all – helped victims ☐
- nation's apology → start of healing / turning point ☐
- think of families never reunited ☐
- remember those – suicide ☐
- mustn't let it happen again ☐

3 Make notes in a grid

[◎] [▤] *You are going to listen to another part of Kevin Rudd's speech. In this extract he outlines measures which will be taken in addition to the apology.*

Think what these measures could be. Make a grid like the following. Then listen to the text and make short notes about the measures Kevin Rudd mentions in his speech.

TIP
It doesn't matter if some of your ideas do not turn up. Leave some empty lines in your grid for topics you weren't expecting.

Measures	Details

4 Write a checklist

[◎] Louise is talking on the phone to Carl Murphy from 'Runaway Children' because she is thinking of volunteering. He tells her everything she needs to know before starting on a training course for volunteers.
What notes does she make (e.g. problems dealt with, help offered, …)?

Listen to the dialogue and complete her checklist.

Guessing the meaning → S32

1 Phrasal verbs

TIP
Phrasal verbs consist of a verb plus at least one more word (usually a preposition and / or an adverb). The meaning can be quite different from the meaning of the basic verb. Phrasal verbs are particularly common in informal language.

Example: He turned the sound down. (reduced)
He turned the offer down. (refused)

TIP
Read the whole text before you start guessing.

a) *Read what this teenage girl says about her first experience of public speaking. Try to guess the meaning of the underlined phrasal verbs from the context.*

"Our school debating society organized a debate about 'A fair society' last month. I had never made a formal speech before, and I didn't want to this time, either, but I couldn't find an excuse to get out of it. While I was doing research for my speech, I came across some really useful information about social change on a music website, of all places! I wasn't expecting that. I decided to talk about the way in which society is unfair to some minorities. I needed a few striking examples, so my audience would understand what I was getting at. I found some impressive stories about families who manage to get by with very little money. Reports like that would go down well with my listeners. At the debate Finley was the first to speak. I was waiting for him to start on the subject of police discrimination. – He always brings that up, no matter what we're talking about. After Finley it was my turn. I was scared stiff when I started to speak, but surprisingly that feeling soon wore off. I looked round anxiously at the audience to make sure they weren't dropping off, but no – they seemed interested. I just hoped they would back me up when it came to the vote at the end. After a few minutes I started to feel confident because I knew that I had important things to say. For my final sentences I decided to do away with my notes and just tell the audience what I felt."

b) *Match the phrasal verbs from a) with these more formal expressions.*

to impress	____________	to fall asleep	____________
to disappear	____________	to discover	____________
to avoid	____________	to throw out	____________
to survive	____________	to mention	____________
to mean	____________	to support	____________

c) [◎] *Now listen to part of the girl's speech. You will hear some phrasal verbs. Find and write down those which mean approximately the same as these verbs and phrases. (You will hear them in this order.)*

separate into sections ____________

not have anything left ____________

educate ____________

reduce consumption ____________

make an informal visit ____________

not fulfil expectations ____________

2 Difficult words and structures

a) *Read Emma's e-mail to her friend Josh.*

> Josh – You asked me about 'MSF' – Médecins Sans Frontières. They're called 'Doctors Without Borders' in some countries, and they provide medical help for people who need it all over the world. They don't take sides, but they don't keep quiet, either! I really admire them. Here's the link to a news report about the MSF.

b) *Before you listen to part of the news report about the MSF, think about what information you expect to hear. Will the language be formal or casual?*
Listen to the whole text and write down the gist in a few words.

____

____

c) [◎] *Now guess the meaning of some words and phrases in the text. Listen carefully and stop the CD after each word from the list. (They are in chronological order.) Use the strategies you know for guessing unknown words (word families, similar words in German, …).*

Concentrate on the parts of the context that you understand. Then write down what the unknown word could mean in German (several possibilities, if you like).

English phrase	Possible meaning
pursues a policy	____________
the scale of atrocities	____________
were outraged by the inability	____________
by bringing abuses to light	____________
making those that watched complicit	____________

d) [◎] *When you have dealt with all the words in c), listen to the text again. Then use a dictionary to check your results.*

Mediation → S34

1 Summarize the main ideas

a) [◎] *Before you listen, read the Fact file about prisoners and the right to vote in the USA. Then listen to a radio commentary on the same topic. Write down the main ideas in your own words.*

FACT FILE

Only two states, Maine and Vermont, allow prisoners to vote. Some states allow criminals to vote once they have been released from prison, even if they are on probation or parole. Others, including Maryland, don't allow voting until the sentence has been fully served.

b) [◎] *Listen again. How is the text divided up into sections? (Pauses? Changes in intonation? Keywords?) Make notes.*

c) *Briefly summarize each section in German for someone who has not heard the text.*

Section 1:

Section 2:

Section 3:

2 Interpreting: Helping people to talk to each other

Tommy, a new American student at your school, is having problems with some teenagers at the sports club he has just joined. He has asked you to help him to talk to the coach about it.

Before you listen, think about your role.

- Is it an easy situation, or do you expect problems?
- Is it important to translate every word?
- What type of language (formal / casual) should you expect and use yourself?
- Should you try to help the people to find solutions, should you take sides – or should you stick to translating and summarizing?

3 Prepare yourself for the situation

[◎] *Listen to the whole dialogue to prepare yourself for your role as 'interpreter'. You can make notes if you like.*

4 Act as interpreter

[◎] *Stop the recording after each speaker and tell the other person in his own language what was said. (Do you need to revise what you decided in ex. 3?)*

Using verbs correctly →G2

To understand a listening text correctly, it is important to know the function of the different tenses used by the speaker(s).

TIP
- The progressive forms are usually used with verbs that describe an action or development in progress (dynamic verbs). Verbs that describe a state (stative verbs) can usually only be used in the simple form.
- Some verbs are not normally used in the progressive form (hear, believe, want, belong).
- Some verbs can be used in both forms but with a difference in meaning (have, look).

1 Using simple and progressive forms of the present tense

a) *The pictures show volunteers in Africa and South America. Describe what is happening in the pictures.*

b) [▤] *Use the information from the pictures and your own imagination to write about a volunteer's life.*

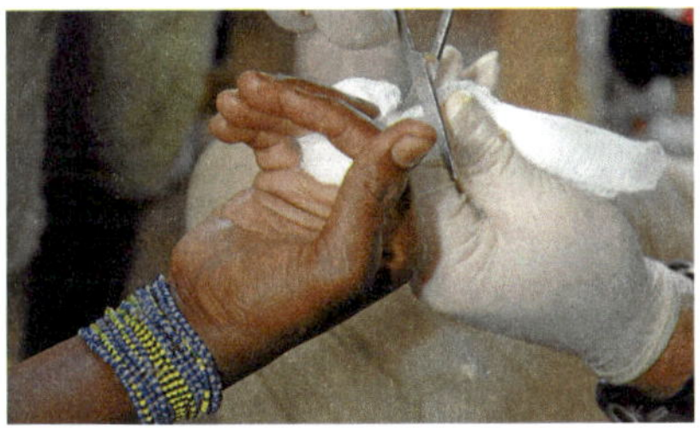

2 The past tense – simple and progressive

[⊡] *Read how Taylor, a young volunteer, came to join the Peace Corps and fill in the correct form of the past tense.*

Even as a child Taylor __________ (read) eagerly everything he could find about the Peace Corps and __________ (dream) of helping the underprivileged of the world, just like the volunteers __________ (do) in their promotional films. He __________ (never • get) tired of watching the young Americans who __________ (smile) cheerfully all the time they __________ (work) in the most awful living conditions. But his serious interest in the organization __________ (develop) one summer vacation when Taylor __________ (work) for a local charity which __________ (distribute) food to the city's poor. When he __________ (leave) college, Taylor __________ (apply) to join the Peace Corps, but at that time they __________ (not take) on any new volunteers. So Taylor __________ (start) a job with an airline. – He __________ (see) that as a chance to travel and to gain work experience. He __________ (keep) up his local volunteer work, and just when he __________ (begin) to give up hope, the Peace Corps __________ (invite) him to spend two years in Paraguay. They __________ (plan) a new health center there, and they __________ (look) for people who spoke Spanish – and Taylor __________ (do).

3 Giving an interview – present perfect simple and present perfect progressive

[👥] [▤] *A journalist wants to interview Taylor for her news programme. In advance she has sent Taylor this list of topics she wants to talk to him about.*

With your partner work out the dialogue between Taylor and the journalist. Use the forms of the present perfect as often as is suitable. Then record your interview and discuss it. Was your use of the verb forms correct?

- Have you always been interested in …?
- Yes, I have, since high school. I worked …

- How long – in S. America / in this village?
- your relevant interests
- Your qualifications: language, healthcare, …
- Most important decisions / experience

Revision for tests 1: Growing up – Friendships

Facebook and the generation gap

Facebook is now bigger than Google. In the US, more people now visit the social networking site to write on each other's walls and swap pictures of parties than turn to Google to get travel directions or check the spelling of 'definitely'.

Social networking, it seems to me, is the biggest separator of the young from the not-so-young. In most other respects there is not much to choose between people of 50 and of 15, apart from a bit of experience and a great many wrinkles. Everyone wears jeans. More or less everyone (quite) likes Florence and the Machine. But 15-year-olds live on Facebook, while 50-year-olds don't understand it at all.

This isn't a small thing: It's an enormous non-meeting of minds between two generations over what is not just a different way of communicating, but a different way of living.

Google is natural for old people, because we were taught how to look things up at primary school. It is like a library, only a lot better: you don't have to get on a bus, and the thing you want is never out on loan to someone else. E-mail is natural for us, too. We might still grapple with the right style for this flat medium, but we understand the principle perfectly. One person communicates with another, only it happens faster than a postman takes to drop a letter through a door.

My generation can even do Twitter – if we really have to. Twitter is just a sort of showing off, and we are just as good at that as anyone born a decade or two after us.

But Facebook remains deeply alien. For us, the point about communicating is that it is an activity between two people. I like to talk to one friend at a time, which allows you to vary the tone and content to suit the person

to whom you are talking. When we deal with more than one or two friends at a time, we get nervous.

By contrast, the idea that communication becomes a random broadcast to 500 'friends' about what you were up to last night is perfectly incomprehensible. As is the thought that you park yourself for hours on end in front of a screen watching the random communications of your unmanageably large group of friends and commenting on them.

I have asked my children to explain Facebook to me, but I'm none the wiser. They can't explain it because they don't understand what I'm asking. The scale of my puzzlement makes no sense to them.

Whether or not we see the point of it, my generation is going to have to sign up in time. A friend of my daughter's recently complained that because her grandfather wasn't on Facebook, she couldn't wish him a happy birthday. The thought of picking up the phone, let alone buying a card, had not occurred to her. If in the future we want to get birthday cards (or communicate with anyone under 40) we are going to have to join Facebook whether we understand it or not.

1 Understanding the text

a) *Tick (✓) the right answers.*

1. How does the author compare 50-year-olds to 15-year-olds?
   a) They wear different clothes and listen to different music. ☐
   b) The biggest difference is that the older people have more wrinkles. ☐
   c) Social networking is a link between the two generations. ☐

2. What does the older generation think of Facebook?
   a) Facebook is nothing that concerns them in their everyday life. ☐
   b) They think that it is unnatural to read the details of your friends' private lives. ☐
   c) Facebook is a great puzzle to the older generation. ☐

3. Google …
   a) requires skills that the older generation learnt in primary school. ☐
   b) is cheap because you need not pay for a bus ride to the library. ☐
   c) is as good as a library. ☐

4. It is the author's conclusion …
   a) that the over 40-year-olds will have to sign up with Facebook, too, in order to communicate. ☐
   b) that the younger people should communicate with the older generation by phone or by post. ☐
   c) that the over 40-year-olds should teach the younger ones how to write birthday cards. ☐

b) [▤] *Using the information from the text, make a list of all the similarities and differences between today's 15-year-olds and 50-year-olds.*

2 Listening: Facebook and a test of friendship

a) [◎] *Listen to a radio programme about social networking sites. Tick (✓) the right answers.*

1. Today's children …
   a) will have spent 20,000 hours online by the time they have grown up. ☐
   b) will have spent most of their online time on social networks. ☐
   c) are called 'Generation Internet'. ☐

2. The founder of Facebook …
   a) was a student at Yale university. ☐
   b) found 1,000 people who joined the network within a day. ☐
   c) wanted to find a way to stay connected with his student friends. ☐

3. Some critics of Facebook say …
   a) that it makes friendship meaningless. ☐
   b) that total strangers can become friends. ☐
   c) both of the above. ☐

4. The speaker mentions a test that was carried out by …
   a) a well-known fast-food chain. ☐
   b) a 40-year-old writer. ☐
   c) a research team in 2009. ☐

5. The test showed that …
   a) people don't think very much of their Facebook friends, so the speaker compares friends with hamburgers. ☐
   b) a great number of people were willing to give up some of their Facebook friends for a free hamburger. ☐
   c) 233,906 people said they could each find 10 friends to go to one certain fast-food restaurant on one particular night. ☐

b) [◎] [▤] *Sum up what the man interviewed at the end of the programme says about the test.*

3 Writing: Living without modern communication?

[▤] *"Mobile phones, WLAN, Skype, Twitter – today's young generation cannot bear to be completely alone." Note down arguments for and against this statement and write your own comment.*

4 Speaking: Setting priorities

[👥] [▤] *What is more important to you – your friends or your parents? Make notes and discuss with a partner.*

5 Mediation: Growing together as a group

[▤] *An American friend shows great interest in the German school system. Tell him what a comprehensive school in Hamburg offers to their students and what the students learn from their 'challenge'. Make notes on the most important information first.*

Helden auf Bewährung

An der Hamburger Gesamtschule Winterhude gehört das Konzept „Herausforderungen“ zum Lehrplan. Für die Jahrgangsstufen 8 bis 10 bietet die Schule jedes Jahr ein dreiwöchiges Abenteuer an, z. B. eine Überquerung der Alpen zu Fuß.

Erfolg oder Scheitern war von Anfang an ihr eigenes Problem. Sogar das Geld mussten die Schüler selbst beschaffen. Der Einsatz der Eltern war auf 150 Euro beschränkt; das reichte kaum für die Zugfahrt. 3000 Euro fehlten der Gruppe noch, knapp kalkuliert. Mit Spendenbüchsen und Kuchenverkauf trieben die Schüler die Summe ein. Einer Apotheke luchsten sie einen Satz Blasenpflaster ab.

Unterwegs kamen dann die echten Krisen. Schon bald lernten die Jungalpinisten, wie schwer es ist, im Hochgebirge cool zu bleiben. Marvin zum Beispiel, Typ Skater, lief die ersten Tage standesgemäß mit offenen Schnürsenkeln. Er büßte mit schweren Blasen und gab nach.

Auch bei den anderen wackelte der Reihe nach die Fassade. Früher oder später hatte jeder mal einen Anfall von Schwäche oder Mutlosigkeit. Oder einfach nur Angst vor einem schwindelerregend steilen Wegstück. Noch heute schwärmen die Kinder vom Rückhalt in der Gruppe. Dort fanden sie Trost und Zuflucht – und sei es nur vor der gelegentlichen Langeweile des Dahinstiefelns. „Dann haben wir eben gesungen“, sagt Juliana.

Nach der Rückkehr bekamen die Schüler Fragebögen. Sie sollten eintragen, was das Abenteuer ihnen gebracht habe. Da steht jetzt unter anderem:

selbstständig sein, weitermachen, in schwierigen Situationen ruhig bleiben, nicht aufgeben, zusammenarbeiten, mit wenig Geld auskommen, Unterkünfte suchen, Rucksack richtig packen, nie zu schnell gehen.

Christoph hat jetzt einen neuen Blick auf die Probleme des Lebens, nämlich von oben: „Mann, du hast die Alpen überquert,“ sagt er sich dann. „Das kriegst du jetzt wohl auch noch hin.

Der Spiegel, 4. April 2010 (gekürzt)

Revision for tests 2: The Blue Planet

Outdoor adventures

Adventure Treks summer adventure programs for young people ages 12 to 18 will be the greatest summer of your life! You'll meet great new friends, learn leadership, gain confidence and challenge yourself through exciting outdoor activities. With 24 students and 6 instructors on each trip, we are able to divide into small groups for many activities. This way, you are challenged at an appropriate level, and you don't have to worry about being too fast or too slow for the rest of the group! Here are some of our exciting wilderness activities:

Rock climbing

Whether you're an expert climber or you've never been rock climbing before, you'll experience a thrilling climb (and a great view from the top) on almost all of our trips. Our trips feature one or two days of climbing in some of the most famous sites in North America, like Smith Rock and Skaha bluffs. We'll set up easy, medium and difficult routes so you'll get enough challenge for any skill level, and you'll be able to climb as many routes as you like.

Sailing

Learn to captain your own sailboat on scenic Klamath Lake, the largest natural lake west of the Rockies during our three-day sailing trips. With 3–5 students and one instructor in each crew, you'll get plenty of hands-on experience as you learn to rig, sail, and even captain your boat! You'll cook meals and sleep on board the boat. The northern part of the lake is a wildlife refuge, so you'll get to see lots of rare marine birds, plants and animals as you explore.

Mountaineering

A typical mountaineering day begins as early as 2 am! You'll begin your hike in the dark, and you might get to see the sunrise over the mountains as you ascend. You and your summit team will reach the top before lunch. But the adventure isn't over yet! Slide on the snow for high-speed, thrilling fun. On trips with multi-day summit attempts, we will teach you to use an ice-axe and crampons for snow travel. On some of the mountains, we'll also show you how to travel as a rope team.

Caving

Only on our Blue Ridge trips will you be able to experience the underground world of caving. You'll put on your helmet and headlamp and crawl, climb, slide, and slog through a muddy, amazing environment. It can be a spooky; turn out your lights to experience total darkness and complete silence! And it can be intense, too. The climbs and drops throughout the cave make it tons of fun. Help your group navigate their way back out as you try to travel the maze of tunnels and hallways.

1 Understanding the text

a) *Decide if these sentences are right or wrong. Correct the wrong sentences.*

1. The activities are for people of all ages.
2. Adventure Treks offers one-to-one courses for different outdoor activities.
3. Students are grouped according to level so that you don't have to worry about your skills.
4. You will be left behind in the wilderness with a group of other students.
5. The courses teach you how to lead a group and gain self-confidence.

b) *Make a grid like the following and collect the information about the different adventure activities (not all the information is provided for each activity).*

	Rock climbing	Mountaineering	Sailing	Caving
Length of course				
Activities offered				
Overall goals				

2 Writing: An adventure trip diary

[▤] *Living in the wilderness without a bathroom, a computer and a TV: Write the diary entry of a teenager on his/her third day of a wilderness trip.*

3 Speaking: Environment or technology ... or both?

[👥] *Do you think it is better to rediscover one's natural environment or to develop more advanced technology? Make notes and discuss with a partner.*

4 Listening: The consequences of oil spills

a) [◎] *You are going to hear part of a discussion about the consequences of oil spills. First read the following statements. Then listen and tick (✓) the correct answers.*

	Right	Wrong
1. Mr. North argues that in the case of former oil spills the fears of the environmentalists proved to be right.	☐	☐
2. He explains that nature recovered after a couple of years.	☐	☐
3. He goes on to say that it is very important to start clean-up activities after an oil spill.	☐	☐
4. Charlie Kronick from Greenpeace points out that in the case of Exxon Valdez, some wildlife communities are still threatened 40 years after the accident.	☐	☐
5. Kronick stresses that the damage to the environment is not just caused by the oil spill as one single event, but also by a larger variety of factors.	☐	☐

b) [◎] [▤] *Correct the wrong statements.*

5 Mediation: Our dependence on oil

[▤] *A British exchange student has read this article in a German newspaper. He tells you that he understands a few words (energy – US coast – Mount Everest – civilization – existence), but that the article doesn't make any sense to him. With the help of the terms above, explain to your exchange partner the main points the author is trying to make.*

Grenze des Machbaren

Ohne Energie wäre der Lebensstil nicht möglich, den die westlichen Länder genießen. Strom für das Licht, Öl für das Auto und Gas für die Heizung erlauben es dem Menschen, Kraft und Kreativität auf Ziele jenseits der blanken Existenzsicherung zu richten.

Er überschätzt dabei aber schnell seine Macht über die Technik und unterschätzt, was er alles nicht weiß. Jeder Fehler kann fatale Folgen für Leib, Leben und Umwelt haben. Je größer die Anlagen, desto weiter reichen die Konsequenzen, wenn Mensch oder Technik versagen.

Die Widersprüche zeigen sich besonders deutlich an der Bohrinsel *Deepwater Horizon*, die am 20. April 2010 im Golf von Mexiko explodiert und dann gesunken ist. Sie symbolisiert technischen Triumph und Umweltkatastrophe gleichermaßen. (...) Acht Monate zuvor hatte diese Bohrinsel Geschichte geschrieben. Unter 1259 Metern Wasser und 9426 Metern Fels war die Mannschaft damals auf Öl gestoßen – das ist, als würde man vom Gipfel des Mount Everest aus einen Kilometer unter den Meeresspiegel bohren. Der Schauplatz der Rekordbohrung, das Tiber-Wells-Ölfeld, liegt etwa 500 Kilometer westlich vom Macondo-Gebiet, aus dem nach der Explosion täglich einige Millionen Liter Rohöl ins Meer strömten. Hier schrieb die Bohrinsel erneut Geschichte, weil sie vermutlich die schwerste Umweltkatastrophe der USA ausgelöst hat.

Seit die Menschheit das Feuer gezähmt hat, nutzt sie Energiequellen an der Grenze des technisch

Beherrschbaren. Das hat Kultur und Zivilisation vorangetrieben, den Wohlstand gemehrt. Aber immer wieder gerieten Menschen auf die falsche Seite der Grenzlinie und verloren Leben oder Lebensunterhalt. Längst haben die Anlagen dabei Dimensionen erreicht, in denen sie ganze Küstenregionen oder – im Fall von Kernkraftwerken – halbe Kontinente bedrohen. (...)

Süddeutsche Zeitung, 3 Mai 2010 (gekürzt)

Speaking activities for test purposes

1 Challenges at high school

a) [ ] ***Informal discussion:*** *Imagine your school offers three-week 'challenges' as part of their curriculum (see Mediation, page 67). Each of you can choose a project from the list on the right.*

You and your friend want to join a project together. Study the list, discuss each of the ideas and agree on a project that you would both like to join. If you want, you can come up with your own ideas.

- planning and building a school café
- organizing a pop concert (including public relations, insurance, etc.)
- running a company that offers support to elderly people, e. g. shopping, garden work, etc.
- renovating an old house and turning it into a guest house for future school trips
- organizing an outdoor adventure trip

b) ***Statement for an interview:*** *Schools or other educational institutions often test the applicants' motivation in a formal interview before accepting them for a programme. Imagine that you have to go to such an interview to join one of the projects listed above. You are expected to give a short statement about why you want to join.*
Make sure that you provide answers to the following questions:

- Why are you interested in this particular project?
- Which useful skills and qualifications can you offer for this project?

As part of your preparation, you can write down your statement, but you cannot use your notes during the interview. Make sure that your statement is about two minutes long so as to really convince the interviewers.

c) ***Tell a story (unprepared):*** *Think about a personal challenge that you dealt with successfully. Tell the story with all its important details, and also tell your listeners what you learned from it.*

2 Islam in Britain

a) ***Statement (prepared):*** *In the story* My son the fanatic *(pages 34–36 in your book), the young man Ali claims that people in the West are too materialistic. Prepare a short comment.*

b) [ ] ***Informal discussion:*** *In Islamic countries, the opinion about Western lifestyle is often based on what is presented on Western TV channels. With a partner, say what this opinion might be and what could be done about it.*

3 Make a difference

a) [ ] ***Panel discussion:*** *Choose six speakers and one chairman / chairwoman. Each of the six speakers delivers a prepared statement on a person who has made a difference (for ideas refer to pages 80–81 and pages 88–89 in your book or research your own ideas). Then discuss who should be awarded a symbolic trophy for having made the greatest difference. The chairman / chairwoman is responsible for opening and closing the discussion and for the speaking order; he or she may also accept questions and contributions from the audience.*

b) [ ] ***Role play:*** *Two teenagers from Europe are planning to take a gap year after school, but they have different ideas about how to spend their year off. Choose one of the roles and prepare yourself by making notes first.*

Partner A

After hearing about people who have made a difference, you would like to go to Africa to do some volunteer work there. Your friend, however, is sceptical. He / She would rather spend the time travelling. Try to convince your friend to join you.

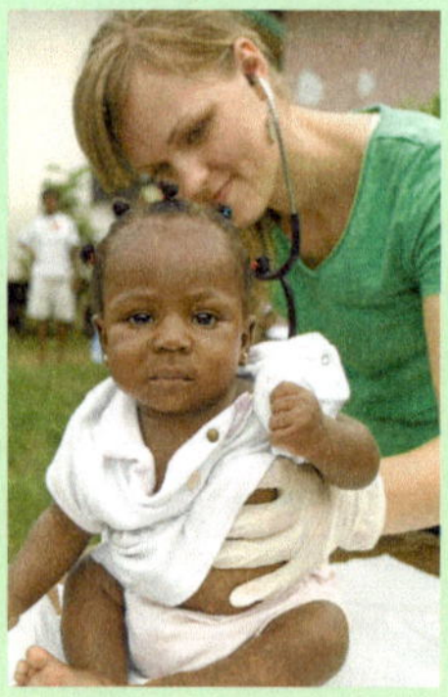

Partner B

You know a number of other high school graduates who went travelling around the world and who met all kinds of different people. Your friend, however, would rather do some volunteer work. Try to convince your friend to join you on your world trip.

4 Fighting the Aids epidemic in South Africa

Formal discussion: *How would you go about fighting the Aids epidemic in South Africa? Imagine the WHO (World Health Organization) set aside US $10 million for a campaign to prevent the further spread of Aids in South Africa. You are members of a government committee that is to discuss how the money should best be spent. Here are four possible roles:*

A politician addressing the public on the prevention of Aids

A teacher trying to inform students about the dangers of contracting HIV

A doctor working for a clinic which provides free anti-Aids drugs

A public figure like a football star warning the public about the epidemic

Choose a chairman / chairwoman who will open and close the meeting and enforce the speaking order if necessary. Discuss the pros and cons of each suggestion first. Come to a joint agreement on what you consider the two most effective strategies. Maybe you have more ideas on your own.

In a second step discuss how to spend the US $10 million most effectively.

5 The environment

a) ***Informal discussion:*** *You and your parents are having breakfast and you discuss the different possibilities of how to spend your summer holidays. You want to go on an adventure trip, while your parents want you to join them on a family holiday.*

Choose one of the roles and note down possible arguments. Then try to convince the other side of your holiday plans. If you can't agree on one of the two suggestions, try to find some activity every family member is happy with.

b) ***Formal debate:*** *What do you think is more important: protecting our natural environment or securing jobs? Note down arguments and examples to support your position.*

c) ***Statement (unprepared):*** *The cost of oil has been rising steadily. How do you think your life will change if oil becomes so expensive (e.g. €10 for a litre of petrol) that only the very rich can continue their lives as before? Give a short statement.*

6 A council meeting

Class discussion: *There is a big, empty plot of land in your community. Different interest groups have formed to try and push their project for this land through the city council. Read the list of projects on the right.*

Form five groups in your class for the five different projects. Each group collects arguments for one of the projects. Choose one chairman / chairwoman to open and close the council meeting and to enforce the speaking order.

During the discussion try and convince the others of the benefits of your project for the community as a whole. End the meeting with a vote on the five projects.

- Don't develop the plot at all. Leave it in its natural state to leave space for family and other activities.
- Build a mosque for the Muslim community.
- Donate it to the local school so students can take part in projects to garden it / build on it / be responsible for it.
- Sell it to a global company for their industrial expansion so that hundreds of new jobs will be created in the area.
- Build a local museum that honours citizens who have made a difference.

Mock exam 1: Multi-ethnic societies

Text 1: Battle for Britain's largest mosque

A Muslim missionary group is hoping to build Britain's biggest mosque on the site of a former chemicals factory in east London. The project has not even left the drawing board, but it has already run into controversy. Despite its rustic sounding name the Abbey Mills Mosque is in the heart of London's East End. Every two minutes it shakes as a train stops at the West Ham Tube station next door.

But inside the atmosphere is one of quiet reverence. The neatly arranged prayer mats and the prayer niche facing Mecca give it a timeless feel. Outside it is showing its age. The ramshackle brick building is all that is left of a demolished chemical factory. Despite this, up to 3,500 Muslims a week come here to pray and discuss their faith.

The missionary group which owns it, Tablighi Jamaat, now wants to replace it with a giant mosque with room for 12,000 people. It hopes that as Britain's biggest mosque it will be a beacon for Muslims across the country – even for foreign visitors to the 2012 London Olympics, which is due to be held a stone's throw away in Stratford.

But some local residents are worried about the impact of such a huge place of worship. Some unflattering newspaper reports have described the planned building as a "megamosque".

"That's an exaggeration." says Faisal Iqbal, a Tablighi Jamaat trustee. He says: "We do have big plans. But we have a big site – 18 acres. As well as the mosque there will be a school, conference centre and landscaped garden. The mosque's maximum capacity will be 12,000. But most weeks there will be fewer than half that number here."

Supporters insist the giant mosque will benefit everyone in the local community – not just Muslims. Its gardens and conference facilities will be open to everyone, they say.

But the plan has attracted fierce criticism from some people in the area. Alan Craig, leader of the Christian People's Alliance, says: "I love the East End's diversity. Tablighi Jamaat preaches separatism by calling Muslims to separate themselves out from the local community. I don't want that to happen here. It's a highly secretive organization and I am suspicious of its motives."

For now the mosque's supporters have promised to consult with local people before submitting the plans for approval. As Mr Iqbal puts it: "No-one is afraid of sports stadiums which hold many times more people. We want to show that this new mosque can be just as much a part of the community as a football ground."

BBC News, March 16, 2008 (abridged)

Assignments:

1 *Summarize the arguments for and against the building of a new mosque.*

2 *Comment on the standpoints presented in the text. In doing so, consider the situation in your own country.*

3 *In a number of European countries some politicians want to ban the full veil (or burqa) in schools and universities. Discuss the pros and cons of this approach.*

Text 2: Controversy over integration in Germany

Streitgespräch über den Bau einer Großmoschee in Köln: Für die Sendung „Streit im Turm" trafen sich der Schriftsteller Ralph Giordano, Gegner des Projekts, und Bekir Alboga, Bundes-Dialogbeauftragter des Bauherrn DITIB (Dachverband Türkisch-Islamische Union) und Referatsleiter für interreligiöse und interkulturelle Zusammenarbeit. Dabei unterhielten sie sich über den Erfolg von Integration in Deutschland.

Journalist: Herr Giordano, Sie haben sich gegen den Bau der Moschee ausgesprochen. Warum?

Giordano: Es ist ein falsches Signal. Wahr ist, dass die Integration der muslimischen Minderheit in Deutschland gescheitert ist. Es wäre ja gut, wenn der Bau einer Moschee genau das Gegenteil ausdrücken würde.

Alboğa: Sie sind völlig falsch informiert. Wir haben mit der Integrationsarbeit doch gerade erst tatkräftig angefangen. Mit dem nationalen Integrationsgipfel der großen Koalition und der Deutschen Islamkonferenz. Die Absicht, dem bestehenden Gotteshaus eine würdige, schöne Form als Moschee zu geben, ist gerade ein Zeichen dafür, dass wir das Gelingen einer Integration in Köln sichtbar machen möchten.

Giordano: Sie sagen, die Integration fängt gerade erst an. Aber es wird seit 25 Jahren darüber gesprochen. Und es hat sich nichts getan. Also ist etwas nicht in Ordnung.

Alboğa: Die Muslime sind kein Fremdkörper in diesem Staat. Es leben rund 3,3 Millionen Muslime in Deutschland, eine Million von ihnen hat die deutsche Staatsangehörigkeit. Wir haben Fußballspieler, Künstler, Schauspieler, Schriftsteller muslimischen Glaubens, die in diese Gesellschaft bestens integriert sind. Man hat jahrelang viel zu lange darüber diskutiert, ob Deutschland ein Einwanderungsland ist oder nicht. Erst jetzt sagt die Regierung: Deutschland ist ein Einwanderungsland geworden. So muss es selbstverständlich sein, dass es Kirchen, Synagogen und auch Moscheen gibt.

Giordano: So geht es nicht. Es ist nicht alles Friede, Freude, Eierkuchen. Ist Ihnen eigentlich entgangen, was in der letzten Zeit an Kritischem über das Zusammenleben von muslimischer Minderheit und nicht-muslimischer Mehrheit gesagt wurde, weil so viel innerhalb der Parallelgesellschaft geschehen ist, das nicht mit dem Grundgesetz in Übereinstimmung zu bringen ist?

Alboğa: Was meinen Sie mit Parallelgesellschaft? Es gibt keine Parallelgesellschaft in Deutschland.

Giordano: Hier leben Muslime, die kein Deutsch können, vor allem Frauen.

Alboğa: Parallelgesellschaft würde bedeuten, dass wir in Deutschland zwei Verfassungen und Grundgesetze hätten. Aber wohin gehen die Menschen, wenn sie Probleme haben? Sie gehen zu einem deutschen Gericht, deutschen Versicherungen, deutschen Schulen, deutschen Universitäten. Wir sind ein selbstverständlicher Teil dieser Gesellschaft mit unseren Identitäten, wie Sie auch ihre Identität haben. Wir dürfen die Meinung der Rechtsradikalen in Deutschland nicht mit falschen Impulsen stärken.

Journalist: Wenn man einen Integrationsprozess will, muss man ehrlich miteinander umgehen. Also muss man benennen, dass es in diesem Land immer noch eine Vielzahl von Menschen gibt, die nicht integriert sind. Was stört Sie an dem Begriff der Parallelgesellschaft?

Alboğa: Ich lade Sie zu uns in die Moschee ein, damit ich Ihnen zeigen kann, welche Integrationsarbeit wir tun. Wir machen Deutschkurse, Integrationskurse und Hausaufgabenbetreuung. Wenn wir keine Integration wollten, bräuchten wir keine Deutschkurse. Wir haben kein Interesse an der Entwicklung einer Parallelgesellschaft. Die Muslime leben seit 45 Jahren in Deutschland. In den ersten 25 Jahren dachte jeder, sie kehren zurück. Bleiben 20 Jahre. Was sind 20 Jahre in der Entwicklung der Menschheit?

Kölner Stadt-Anzeiger, 16. Mai 2007 (gekürzt)

Assignment:

Imagine you are working as an intern for a British anti-racist group. One of your tasks is to search the Internet for articles about the state of integration in Germany. Write an English summary of the interview above for your British colleagues.

Mock exam 2: Make a difference

Text 1: Rosa Parks – one of the 100 most important people of the 20th century

"Individually we could do nothing. So we formed a committee which determined nothing could be done."

Rosa Parks was a very ordinary woman, a seamstress working for a department store in Montgomery, Alabama. What made her famous, though, was a very extraordinary and a very courageous decision she took one evening. She simply did nothing – or maybe it would be more accurate to say she refused to do as she was told. This in turn led to her arrest, which resulted in a mass protest, which changed the course of history. So what exactly did she do or rather not do?

On Thursday, 1 December 1955, 42-year-old Rosa Parks boarded a bus after a long day's work to go home. She did what every black citizen in Montgomery was required to do by law: she got on the bus at the front, paid her fare, and got off the bus again only to re-enter it through the back door because blacks were not allowed to walk through the section reserved for whites. She was lucky that evening, for sometimes the bus set off before the black customers had made it to the back door. She found an empty seat in the section designated for blacks and was glad that she could give her sore feet some rest.

After a couple of stops the bus filled up. There were no seats left. Back in 1955 that meant in Montgomery that as soon as a white person was looking for a seat, all the blacks sitting in one row had to make room – because a white person could not be expected to sit next to or even across the aisle from a black person. The bus driver told the black passengers, including Rosa Parks, to get up or else he would have them arrested. Everybody did as they were told, except for Rosa Parks. She just remained seated.

Later she said in an interview that she didn't realize then that her decision would spark a whole movement, she only refused to get up because she had come to the sudden realization that it was outrageous how blacks were treated in Alabama. But, alas, the law being the law, the bus driver called a policeman to have Rosa Parks arrested for her violation of the segregation laws.

On the very next day the protest against her arrest and against the discriminating bus laws began to take shape. The black population of Montgomery was urged to boycott the city buses from the following Monday on, to stay out of school, to walk or to take a black cab. Monday came and although it rained, no black person was seen on board any of the city's busses.

The Montgomery bus boycott went on for weeks and months because 17,000 African-Americans were united in their protest. The bus company was losing money, the shops in the downtown area realized that more and more blacks were shopping closer to home and the shops were also making losses. Eventually, a year after Rosa Parks' arrest the US Supreme Court ruled that the Montgomery bus laws were unconstitutional. That was the beginning of the civil rights movement in the United States.

On the day after the court ruling, Rosa Parks was one of the first to board a city bus again and this time she sat in the front row.

Assignments:

1 *Sum up the events in December 1955 and after.*

2 *Explain why the Montgomery bus laws discriminated against blacks.*

3 *Compare the message of the text and the cartoon.*

4 *Choose one of the following tasks:*

a) *Comment on the standpoints presented in the text and the cartoon.*

b) *In the role of a representative for a major aid organization, write a speech for an international conference about the importance of individuals making a difference.*

Text 2: A German student plays football to fight Aids

Sebastian Neuerburg trainiert kleine Township-Fußballer für ein besseres Leben. Der 25-jährige Student der Sporthochschule Köln arbeitet seit zwei Monaten als Freiwilliger für eine südafrikanische Non-Profit-Organisation, die Sportunterricht für Kinder und Jugendliche aus den Townships organisiert. Seit 2007 kicken täglich an die 120 Jungsportler auf dem Platz in einem 15.000-Einwohner-Ort unweit von Kapstadt.

Das Fußballprojekt ist Arena für einen wichtigen Kampf: gegen Aids. Zwar liegt die Rate in der westlichen Kapregion deutlich unter dem Landesdurchschnitt von 18 Prozent, infiziert sind aber immer noch zu viele. Durch Rollenspiele und kurze Unterrichtseinheiten im Sitzkreis sprechen die Trainer mit den Kindern über das, was zu Hause oft als Tabu behandelt wird.

Deswegen hat Neuerburg sich durch Videos auf YouTube geklickt und Blogs von Hilfsorganisationen gelesen. Er wollte wissen, wie der Fußball lebenswichtiges Wissen übertragen kann. Eines der Spiele, die er gefunden hat, geht so: Ein paar Kinder schlüpfen in die Rolle von Bakterien, sie versuchen, ihre Gegner mit dem Ball zu treffen. Doch ein anderer Stoßtrupp, das Immunsystem, schützt die Angegriffenen, er wehrt die Bälle ab. Dann kommt das Virus, ein einzelner Spieler. Es schnappt sich die Hände der Lebensretter und behindert sie. Jetzt sind die Kinder in Gefahr, von den Bakterien-Bällen getroffen zu werden. „Und danach reden wir über den Sinn des Spiels“, erzählt Neuerburg.

„Fußball ist hier eindeutig ein Sport der Schwarzen“, sagt Neuerburg. An seinen Teams kann er das täglich beobachten: Sie setzen sich fast ausschließlich aus schwarzen Schülern zusammen. Es sind die, die sich häufig keine Sportschuhe leisten können und meist nicht krankenversichert sind. Viele der jungen Spieler in Neuerburgs Teams träumen davon, eines Tages als Profi-Sportler in der Nationalmannschaft zu spielen. „Es gibt hier wirklich ein paar begnadete Fußballer“, erzählt der Student. Doch nur die wenigsten werden es schaffen, das weiß Neuerburg. Darum hat er seinen Zöglingen in der vergangenen Woche einen Vortrag zum Thema „bekannte Sportgrößen“ gehalten. „Ich habe den Kindern gezeigt, dass fast alle guten Sportler eine Ausbildung oder ein Studium abgeschlossen haben.“

Der Spiegel, 10. Februar 2010 (gekürzt)

Assignment:

Imagine you are Sebastian Neuerburg. A South African newspaper asks you for an interview about your volunteering experience. They also want to know how you became interested in the project. Think of possible questions you might be asked and write the interview.

Bild- und Textquellen

Bildquellennachweis

Umschlag 1.1 Avenue Images GmbH RF (Image Source), Hamburg; **Umschlag 4.1** Getty Images (Stone), München; **1.1** Bananastock, Watlington/Oxon; **4.1** laif (Ruetschi/Keystone), Köln; **5.1** Corbis (Simone Cecchetti), Düsseldorf; **5.2** iStockphoto (Duncan Gilbert), Calgary, Alberta; **6.1** iStockphoto (Arpad Nagy-Bagoly), Calgary, Alberta; **7.1** Alamy Images (Jack Sullivan), Abingdon, Oxon; **7.2** Alamy Images (DBURKE), Abingdon, Oxon; **8.1** Alamy Images (Andry A/Alamsyah), Abingdon, Oxon; **8.2** Alamy Images (flab Istr), Abingdon, Oxon; **9.1** iStockphoto (Don Bayley), Calgary, Alberta; **10.1** Alamy Images (Janine Wiedel Photolibrary), Abingdon, Oxon; **11.1** Avenue Images GmbH RF (Banana Stock), Hamburg; **11.2; 11.3** Alamy Images (Janine Wiedel Photolibrary), Abingdon, Oxon; **13.1** Alamy Images (Stuart Kelly), Abingdon, Oxon; **14.1** iStockphoto (thebroker), Calgary, Alberta; **14.2** Mauritius RF (Kinne), Mittenwald; **15.1** Alamy Images (Heidi James), Abingdon, Oxon; **15.2** laif (Zeng YI/XINHUA/GAMMA/Eyedea Presse), Köln; **16.1** The Associated Press GmbH (National Archives of Australia), Frankfurt am Main; **16.2** Picture-Alliance (EPA/ALAN PORRITT), Frankfurt; **17.1** Dreamstime LLC (Darren Robertson), Brentwood, TN; **18.1** Alamy Images (Jeff Morgan), Abingdon, Oxon; **18.2** Corbis (Tim Pannell), Düsseldorf; **18.3** Thinkstock (Jupiterimages), München; **19.1** iStockphoto (track5), Calgary, Alberta; **19.2** iStockphoto (belterz), Calgary, Alberta; **21.1** iStockphoto (Chris Price), Calgary, Alberta; **22.1** Getty Images (Jun Sato/WireImage), München; **23.1** iStockphoto (ArtisticCaptures), Calgary, Alberta; **24.1** iStockphoto (Linda Yolanda), Calgary, Alberta; **26.1** iStockphoto (naes), Calgary, Alberta; **27.1** Klett-Archiv (Feuerbach), Stuttgart; **28.1** Bananastock, Watlington/Oxon; **30.1** Corbis (Jeff Albertson), Düsseldorf; **30.2** Dreamstime LLC (Lawrence Wee), Brentwood, TN; **30.3** Getty Images (Mick Hutson/Redferns), München; **32.1** Avenue Images GmbH RF (Design Pics RF), Hamburg; **35.1** Alamy Images (Sigrid Olsson), Abingdon, Oxon; **36.1** Alamy Images (Graham Oliver), Abingdon, Oxon; **37.1** Picture-Alliance (Photoshot), Frankfurt; **38.1** Alamy Images (Philip Wolmuth), Abingdon, Oxon; **39.1; 39.2** Imago, Berlin; **40.1** Getty Images, München; **42.1** Imago, Berlin; **42.2** Imago (Camera 4/Jim), Berlin; **42.3** Alamy Images (Ashley Cooper), Abingdon, Oxon; **43.1** Alamy Images (Mohamad Itani), Abingdon, Oxon; **44.1** Corbis (Skyscan), Düsseldorf; **45.1** iStockphoto (David Parsons), Calgary, Alberta; **46.1** Imago, Berlin; **47.1** iStockphoto (Leadinglights), Calgary, Alberta; **50.1** Fotolia LLC, New York; **52.1** Alamy Images (Des Willie), Abingdon, Oxon; **53.1** Picture-Alliance, Frankfurt; **53.2** NETZ www.bangladesch.org (Herold), Wetzlar; **54.1** Getty Images (David Paul Morri), München; **55.1** Picture-Alliance (Julian Stratenschulte), Frankfurt; **56.1** www.cartoonstock.com (Schwadron, Harley), Bath; **56.2** shutterstock (Lisa F. Young), New York, NY; **58.1** Corbis (Vladimir Godnik/moodboard), Düsseldorf; **58.2** Alamy Images (Jeff Greenberg), Abingdon, Oxon; **60.1** shutterstock (Liv friis-larsen), New York, NY; **60.2** iStockphoto (vndr ttn), Calgary, Alberta; **61.1** iStockphoto (Sean Warren), Calgary, Alberta; **61.2** Alamy Images (Paul Harris), Abingdon, Oxon; **62.1** iStockpoto (Monika Wisniewska), Calgary, Alberta; **63.1** iStockphoto (Joerg Reimann), Calgary, Alberta; **64.1** iStockphoto (Geir-Olav Lyngfjell), Calgary, Alberta; **64.2** iStockphoto (robert cocquyt), Calgary, Alberta; **64.3** iStockphoto (technotr), Calgary, Alberta; **64.4** iStockphoto (Michael Ciu), Calgary, Alberta; **65.1** Corbis (Joel W. Rogers), Düsseldorf; **65.2** Corbis (US Coast Guard/Handout), Düsseldorf; **66.1** Corbis (Emely/zefa), Düsseldorf; **66.2** iStockphoto (MShep2), Calgary, Alberta; **66.3** iStockphoto (charles taylor), Calgary, Alberta; **67.1; 67.4** Fotosearch Stock Photography, Waukesha, WI; **67.2** Fotosearch Stock Photography (PhotoDisc), Waukesha, WI; **67.3** Corbis (Simon Jarratt), Düsseldorf; **70.1** www.cartoonstock.com (Hardin, Patrick), Bath

Textquellennachweis

S. 4 http://www.physorg.com; **S. 6** © Clare Wigfall, Penelope Lively und George Szirtes, Picador; **S. 9** © The Observer, Sunday 18 January 2009; **S. 16** © Department of the Prime Minister and Cabinet, Australia, www.pm.gov.au; **S. 18** http://www.guardian.co.uk, 10 September 2008; **S. 20** © copyright 2009. Pew Research Center. Forty Years After Woodstock, A Gentler Generation Gap. http://pewsocialtrends.org/pubs/739/woodstock-gentler-generation-gap-musicby-age; **S. 21** This information was provided by KidsHealth®, one of the largest resources online for medically reviewed health information written for parents, kids, and teens. For more articles like this, visit KidsHealth.org or TeensHealth.org. © 1995- 2010 . The Nemours Foundation/KidsHealth®. All rights reserved.; **S. 22** http://www.direct.gov.uk; **S. 22** http://www.trentfmarenanottingham.com; **S. 23** http://news.bbc.co.uk; **S. 24** Just along for the ride, Dennis Kurumada, aus Sun and shadow, Supplementary Reader in Contemporary American Literature for International Students of English, US Information Agency, Washington, DC, 1972; **S. 26** Copyright © 2010 PsychCentral.com; **S. 27** The Guardian, 4 October 2008; **S. 29** http://www.southwalesargus.co.uk; **S. 32** © Copyright Sunday Times Newspapers Limited, 2010, Virginia Street, London, E98 1XY, December 11, 2005; **S. 42** http://www.foe.co.uk; **S. 57** © Department of the Prime Minister and Cabinet, Australia, www.pm.gov.au; **S. 62** The Financial Times Ltd, London; **S. 63** Der Spiegel, 15/2010; **S. 64** ©2010 Adventuretreks.com; **S. 65** Süddeutsche Zeitung, 03.05.2010,www.sueddeutsche.de; **S. 70** http://news.bbc.co.uk, 16 March 2008; **S. 71** Kölner Stadt-Anzeiger, 16.05.2007, http://www.ksta.de; **S. 73** Der Spiegel, 10.02.2010

Sollte es in einem Einzelfall nicht gelungen sein, den korrekten Rechteinhaber ausfindig zu machen, so werden berechtigte Ansprüche selbstverständlich im Rahmen der üblichen Regelungen abgegolten.